ASTD Training Basics Series

COACHING *Basics*

LISA HANEBERG

A Complete, How-to Guide to Help You:

Understand the Value of Coaching

Create Results-Driven Coaching

Increase Organizational Effectiveness

 **ASTD Press**

ASTD Press is an internationally renowned source of insightful and practical information on workplace learning and performance topics, including training basics, evaluation and return-on-investment (ROI), instructional systems development (ISD), e-learning, leadership, and career development.

Ordering information: Books published by ASTD Press can be purchased by visiting our Website at store.astd.org or by calling 800.628.2783 or 703.683.8100.

Library of Congress Control Number: 2005939031

ISBN-10: 1-56286-424-6
ISBN-13: 978-1-56286-424-8

Acquisitions and Development Editor: Mark Morrow
Copyeditor: April Davis
Interior Design and Production: Kathleen Schaner
Cover Design: Renita Wade
Cover Illustration: Jay Belmore

Printed by Victor Graphics, Baltimore, Maryland. www.victorgraphics.com.

Table of Contents

About the
Training Basics Series

ASTD's *Training Basics* series recognizes and, in some ways, celebrates the fast-paced, ever-changing reality of organizations today. Jobs, roles, and expectations change quickly. One day you might be a network administrator or a process line manager, and the next day you might be asked to train 50 employees in basic computer skills or to instruct line workers in quality processes.

Where do you turn for help? The ASTD *Training Basics* series is designed to be your one-stop solution. The series takes a minimalist approach to your learning curve dilemma and presents only the information you need to be successful. Each book in the series guides you through key aspects of training: giving presentations, making the transition to the role of trainer, designing and delivering training, and evaluating training. The books in the series also include some advanced skills such as performance and basic business proficiencies.

The ASTD *Training Basics* series is the perfect tool for training and performance professionals looking for easy-to-understand materials that will prepare non-trainers to take on a training role. In addition, this series is the perfect reference tool for any trainer's bookshelf and a quick way to hone your existing skills. The titles currently planned for the series include:

- ► *Presentation Basics* (2003)
- ► *Trainer Basics* (2003)
- ► *Training Design Basics* (2003)
- ► *Facilitation Basics* (2004)
- ► *Communication Basics* (2004)
- ► *Performance Basics* (2004)
- ► *Evaluation Basics* (2005)
- ► *Needs Assessment Basics* (2005)
- ► *Return on Investment (ROI) Basics* (2005)
- ► *Organization Development Basics* (2005).

Preface

■ ■

Great coaching can make a world of difference by helping people move mountains. It helps move mountains of self-imposed resistance. It can enable the client to budge mountain-size barriers getting in the way of actions and results. Coaching can simplify wading through mountains of details, ideas, action items, and possibilities. Coaching is a core skill for trainers, managers, organization development practitioners, and human resources professionals.

One of the quickest and most effective ways for you to affect an organization is through coaching. Coaching yields short-term and long-term payoffs. Helping others achieve their goals boosts results today and builds the organization's skills for tomorrow. Unfortunately, coaching is an underused and poorly understood tool. Take the word *coaching*. It means many things to people and is used to describe various conversations:

- ▶ any conversation that helps
- ▶ any conversation between a supervisor and an employee, regardless of the content
- ▶ encouragement or advice
- ▶ weekly addresses by email or phone
- ▶ corrective counseling.

Coaching Basics presents a concept of coaching targeted and focused on helping clients move their goals forward. Although all coaching conversations are helpful, not all helpful conversations are coaching. Coaching conversations often occur between a supervisor and an employee, but most of their conversations do not constitute coaching. Coaches do encourage their clients, but the encouragement itself is not usually coaching. Advice is rarely coaching because it focuses on the advice giver's perspective, not the client's. General speeches or communications can be informative, and some are even catalytic, but without the active involvement of the client, they are not coaching. Corrective counseling focuses on what the supervisor wants, not necessarily on the goals of the client employee and is, therefore, not coaching.

Coaching is a service-oriented practice that is squarely focused on the goals, desires, and intentions of the client. Coaching is often catalytic in nature, meaning that it sparks new thought and action and speeds up results. It is rewarding to provide clients with the coaching that enables them to move goals forward. Knowing what to say, when to say it, and how to say it is part of the challenge of developing your coaching craft.

Who Should Read This Book?

This book covers the basic skills and principles needed to provide effective coaching, and will serve several audiences:

- ▶ trainers who want to do more coaching
- ▶ managers who want to improve their coaching skills
- ▶ organization development professionals at the beginning of their careers
- ▶ human resources professionals who want to build coaching skills.

Coaching Basics offers the theory, techniques, examples, and exercises needed to create a thorough understanding of basic coaching. Readers can use the book's suggestions to begin coaching immediately.

Look for These Icons

This book strives to make it easy for you to understand and apply its lessons. Icons throughout this book help you identify key points.

What's Inside This Chapter

Each chapter opens with a summary of the topics addressed in the chapter. You can use this reference to find the areas that interest you most.

Think About This

These are helpful tips for how to use the tools and techniques presented in the chapter.

Basic Rules

These rules cut to the chase. They represent important concepts and assumptions that form the foundation of coaching.

Noted

This icon calls out additional information.

Getting It Done

The final section of each chapter supports your ability to apply coaching tools and techniques. This section offers suggestions, additional resources, or questions that will help you get started.

Acknowledgments

This book represents a culmination of my 22-year (and counting) practice of coaching. I have benefited from some great coaching myself and would like to thank the following people for being catalysts for me. Thanks to Dave Borden, Jim Booth, Bob Drinane, Ralph Stayer, Charlie Jacobs, Laurie Ford, Jeffrey Ford, Kate Mulqueen, Linda O'Toole, and the many others who have helped shape and expand my coaching practice.

1

What Is Coaching?

■ ■

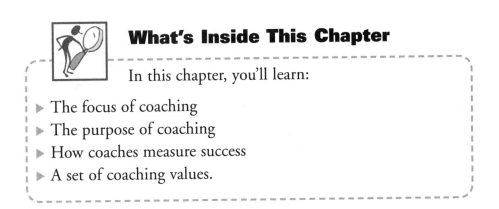

What's Inside This Chapter

In this chapter, you'll learn:

▶ The focus of coaching
▶ The purpose of coaching
▶ How coaches measure success
▶ A set of coaching values.

The Focus of Coaching

Coaching is client focused and goal focused and is often held during one-on-one conversations. Coaching can be used as a catchall phrase for any conversation between two people where the intent is to help. However, coaching is a conversation focused on helping other people (the clients) move forward relative to their goals. Figure 1-1 depicts the focus of coaching.

Noted

The term client *means anyone receiving coaching and can include managers, peers, employees, or others. Coaching is a conversation that exists to help clients reach their goals.*

Notice that coaching focuses on the client's goals, hopes, and curiosities. Goals are unmet accomplishments. Hopes and curiosities are the rough material of future goals. In other words, coaching should concentrate on helping the client move forward with a desire. Coaching is for the benefit of the client. In figure 1-1, the categories that should not be the focus of coaching include what others want, to-do list, and client's failures. For coaching to be helpful, it needs to tie in to something the client wants to accomplish. Topics may be represented in more than one place. For example, a to-do list item may also be one of the client's goals. If it's a goal, then coaching about this topic can be worthwhile.

Many people confuse coaching with advice and other business conversations. If coaching were that broad, this would need to be a much bigger book called *How to Communicate.* When you give advice, it may not be welcome and the conversation

Figure 1-1. The focus of coaching.

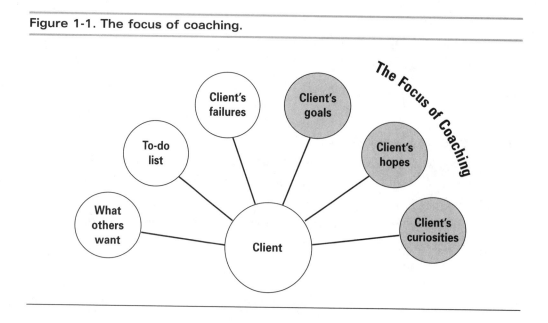

centers on your opinion or perspective. When you provide coaching, the focus is on the other person and the goals that person wants to discuss. The phrase, "Can I give you some coaching?" is often followed with advice and rarely results in coaching.

Basic Rule 1
Coaching should focus on the client's goals, hopes, and curiosities.

Coaching is also different from preaching, counseling, and persuading because these conversations come from your point of view and serve your goals, not the client's. Coaching is the exact opposite. A great coach talks little, listens a lot, and facilitates the client's thinking process. The difference between a coaching conversation and a general business conversation is the focus. A conversation can be about anything. Coaching focuses on the clients and the goals they are trying to accomplish.

The Purpose of Coaching

Forty experienced external and internal coaches were surveyed on several aspects of coaching. Their responses are sprinkled throughout this book. Here are several responses to the question, "What is the purpose of coaching?"

▶ "To help people connect with themselves so they can be better suited to make better decisions about what and how they want to move forward in their lives." Stewart Berman

▶ "To help individuals discover their potentials and achieve that—whatever that is." Bonnie S. Turner

▶ "To lead students to their full potentials." Laurence Haughton

▶ "Coaching creates space to work on a business by taking time away from working in it. It is an opportunity to rise above the day-to-day and work with a trained facilitator to develop new ways of viewing, analyzing, and taking action on opportunities. Coaching provides witness and external accountability." Barry Goldberg

▶ "Enhance and develop skills—life, business, relationship—so that people are happier, more productive, and able to achieve their life-goals in a balanced way." Dave Pughe-Parry

▶ "To allow others to learn self-coaching through multiple perspectives and challenging assumptions." Stan Herman

▶ "To make good things happen sooner." Barry Zweibel

▶ "To keep clients focused on their visions and move them to actions." Paul Lemberg

▶ "To help successful leaders achieve positive, long-term changes in behavior—for themselves, their people, and their teams." Marshall Goldsmith

▶ "To create a partnership that supports profound change and growth through the creation of goals and specific action plans." Christina Madrid

▶ "To help people see themselves—and their situations—more objectively and learn to deal with reality, instead of their fantasies." Adrian Savage

▶ "Helping people to maximize their strengths and manage around their weaknesses." Rosa Say

▶ "To help people be the best that they can be. To help them get really clear about their intentions and wants. And then to catalyze them into action." Lora Adrianse

▶ "To enable and support others in the process of focusing on goals, developing plans, and achieving results." Kathleen Ream

▶ "To help us clear away the muck and muddle so we can see the path ahead, be aware of the obstacles and possible ways around them, and believe that we really have what it takes to make the journey and understand how." Curt Rosengren

These are all positive reasons to coach! Most of the survey responses highlight the service-oriented nature of coaching. It's all about your clients, their needs, their goals, their potential, and their barriers to success. Great coaches feel satisfied and fulfilled when they help others succeed. The survey responses cluster into six purposes of coaching:

1. Coaching should improve client coachability.
2. Coaching should help the client get unstuck.
3. Coaching should enhance client self-awareness.
4. Coaching should facilitate client breakthroughs.
5. Coaching should uncover potential and build client skills.
6. Coaching should help create and implement client plans for action.

This book covers each of these six purposes of coaching. Coaching, often done one-on-one, is a labor- and time-intensive practice. Therefore, it ought to provide substantial benefits, right? Each time you coach a client, one or more of these purposes should be met. Great coaching sessions will satisfy two, three, or more purposes.

Think About This

What do you want from the coaching you receive? Think about the best and worst coaching you have received. What did the great coaching look like? How did the coach behave? What made the worst coaching ineffective? By thinking about your experiences and the needs that have been met by past coaching conversations, you can see examples that will serve your own coaching practice.

How Should Coaches Measure Success?

An important part of building any craft and practice is determining what success looks like. How you measure success affects your focus, beliefs, and actions. When coaching a client, it can be difficult to assess success. Is it when the client is happy with the coaching? Is it when the client listens to and acts on your suggestions? Is it when your coaching proves to be helpful? Are you successful when clients are promoted? Are you a failure if they lose their jobs? None of these measures alone will tell you if your coaching efforts have been a success. Here are a few of the survey responses to the question, "How do you measure your success as a coach?"

- ▶ "Mini-surveys designed to determine degree of progress against goals over a 12- or 18-month period." Mark Sobol
- ▶ "If the people being coached feel that they are taking a path that is right for them, then I have been successful." Bonnie S. Turner
- ▶ "In how much the student can achieve without me." Laurence Haughton
- ▶ "Before I begin working with clients, we look at how they are measured. Assuming there is nothing off in their performance management system, then their success is how mine is measured." Barry Goldberg

Basic Rule 2

The six purposes of coaching are to improve client coachability, help the client get unstuck, enhance client self-awareness, facilitate client breakthroughs, uncover potential and build client skills, and help create and implement client plans for action.

> ► "If my clients express that they see something new or receive value—that's awesome. If change is actually occurring—even if it's simply a change in awareness—that is huge. If the goals that clients set are being achieved or consciously changed." Kathy Bass
>
> ► "I only get paid if my clients achieve positive, long-term, measurable change in leadership behavior—as determined by preselected, key stakeholders." Marshall Goldsmith

These and the other survey responses share a few common themes. Coaching is successful when the client is successful. Coaching is successful when it builds the client's capability for future endeavors. Coaching is successful when the client returns for more coaching or refers others to that coach. Although the ultimate success of coaching should be judged by the results of the client, there are also several smaller, day-to-day coaching successes:

- ► creating an aha moment that leads to a beneficial shift in thinking
- ► conversing that helps the client clarify goals
- ► influencing, in a positive way, the coachability of the client.

Successful coaches make a significant difference to the productivity and success of their clients. They enable change and transformation and facilitate forward movement toward goals.

Basic Rule 3
Coaching is successful when clients are successful in attaining their goals for the coaching.

Success is best measured and defined from the viewpoints of the clients. Your success as a coach is determined by your clients. Sometimes, your clients' peers and managers will also notice the positive change and provide an objective perspective about the difference the coaching has made. Depending on the situation, it might even be the case that your client's manager is also your client if the coaching has been requested and arranged by him or her. Under these situations, it is important to have a clear agreement about the goals and contracting conditions with both parties upfront. Even when requested by their managers, the coaching must always serve the needs of your clients.

Noted

According to Coach U's Essential Coaching Tools, *the things people want most are to make and keep more money, get more done in less time, communicate more effectively, feel better physically and emotionally, increase their quality of life, become closer with others, eliminate hassles, and get on a path toward meeting a goal.*

Important Coaching Skills

Given the focus and purposes of coaching, what are the most important skills for great coaches to possess? The list of beneficial skills would be endless, but it is helpful to know which skills are critical to the role of a coach. Table 1-1 summarizes the survey responses to the question, "What are the two most important skills needed to be a great coach?"

Notice that the largest category of skills is communication. Coaches need to be effective communicators. Among survey participants, listening was the most important skill and was mentioned 81 percent of the time. These experienced coaches noted that deep, active listening is required. The five most mentioned skills were

- listening
- asking the right questions
- being curious
- improving motivation for change or action
- putting aside your personal agenda.

In general, the ability to create great dialogue and be a catalytic force is essential. You will learn more about these areas throughout the rest of this book.

What gets in the way of great coaching? Most coaches are intelligent and well meaning, but they are not all effective. An overreliance on process and protocol can get in the way of the coaching experience and results. If the coach seems more interested in

Table 1-1. Most important skills needed to be a great coach.

Category	Skill
Communication	• Listen • Be direct • Provide feedback • Be empathetic • Ask the right questions • Be quiet • Relate experiences • Provide encouragement • Generate alternatives • Connect information • Engender trust
Client Motivation	• Improve motivation for change or action • Facilitate change/transition • Believe in the client's ability • Improve coachability
Self-Management	• Be curious • Be nonjudgmental • Have humility • Put aside personal agenda • Be self-aware • Be fully present
Technical Skill	• Develop theories of motivation • Implement coaching practices and tools • Increase knowledge of the business • Develop strategies and plans • Contract

following a specific method or is reluctant to skip steps, the client might lose interest or patience. Problems can also occur when the coach is unavailable for ad hoc coaching. It is important not to overschedule your time, thus reducing the opportunities you have to coach. Good chemistry is also a plus. A coach-client relationship will perform better if the chemistry is good. Poor chemistry often leads to the client losing interest in coaching.

Learning the craft of coaching is a lifelong journey. Along with your successes, you will make mistakes and learn a few lessons the hard way. Here are some of the lessons that survey participants learned the hard way:

▶ "I learned a lesson about confidentiality very early in my career. I was coaching a team of executives whose company was being acquired. They were in secret negotiations. One of them mentioned to me that this was occurring. Later that week, I asked one of the other executives about the progress of the negotiations. I had just put the first person in a difficult position because he had not been given permission to share this information with outside persons. The result was that two of us were very embarrassed. The experience taught me the true meaning of the phrase strictest confidence." Mark Sobol

▶ "Over time I've had enough ineffective coaching experiences (both as a coach and as a client) that I've come to realize how important an other-focused outlook is for a coach. When coaches care more about their successes than the clients' successes, things often don't work out quite right." Brendon Connelly

▶ "Coaching is more about questions than answers. One of my clients was struggling with a business challenge that I had a lot of experience solving, and I let myself slip into being a consultant. One cannot coach and consult at the same time." Barry Goldberg

▶ "I didn't listen properly and didn't do a thorough assessment. We were so far apart that we missed each other—we weren't even running parallel!" Dave Pughe-Parry

▶ "I saw the solution to an issue and gave advice. The advice was partially implemented and failed. I was at fault in the client's eyes." Stan Herman

▶ "In my work, I don't get paid if my clients don't achieve positive, measurable change in behavior. I have learned (the hard way) not to work with clients who don't really want to change, not to work with clients whose issues are not connected with my area of expertise (e.g., strategy, technical knowledge), and not to work with clients whose companies or co-workers won't really give them a chance." Marshall Goldsmith

▶ "People can be manipulative, especially if they want you to confirm their stories about what's been going on. Unless you listen extremely carefully, you can find yourself being led along a fool's path." Adrian Savage

▶ "If the issue is about lack of integrity, coaching is not the answer." Carlos Marin

Many of these lessons learned involved the skill of being client-focused versus self-focused. Several survey participants also mentioned that they learned the lesson of not giving clients the answers. It is very tempting to share opinions, ideas, and suggestions. After all, you want to be as helpful as possible. Even so, it is more helpful to listen, ask great questions, and facilitate your client's self-discovery.

Think About This

It can be tough to break the habit of giving answers to clients too quickly (versus allowing them to explore the options), because clients often ask for their coaches' opinions about what they should do. If your client asks for your opinion, say, "I will share my thoughts, but let's first explore all the options and get input from a few other people." Often, the conversation will become lively and active, and you may not need to offer your opinion at all.

Basic Rule 4

Clients seek coaching because it works for them and is a great use of their precious time.

Values Important for Coaching

Values are at the core of your thoughts, actions, and results. Values support the skills you need to fulfill the six purposes of coaching. To be most successful as a coach, you should share the values listed in table 1-2.

By focusing on what your client wants to achieve, you can provide coaching that makes a difference. Great coaches are bold and courageous in one moment and reflective and playful in the next. They adapt their dialogues to be most helpful in moving the client forward.

Getting It Done

Table 1-3 summarizes the points made in this chapter about the nature of great coaching. Review this chart before each of your meetings and coaching conversations. Using this tool as a reminder is a great way to internalize the basic foundation of effective coaching. You can also use table 1-3 to assess your skills and experiences and create a personal development plan.

Table 1-2. Coaching values.

Value	Explanation
Acceptance	Coaches should not try to change the clients' goals or otherwise manipulate the conversations. To be a great coach, you need to accept the clients' goals, intentions, and desires as being worthy and valid.
Adventure	Coaching can be very adventurous when your mind is open and willing to explore diverse avenues and perspectives. Having an adventurous spirit will help your clients move beyond their comfort zones.
Authenticity	Open and authentic communication between coaches and clients is critical to the quality of business solutions and relationships. Systems that promote and reinforce authenticity enable quick problem identification and resolution.
Courage	Sometimes a coach needs to have the courage to ask a difficult question or share a tough observation. Your clients deserve open and candid dialogues presented in a caring manner.
Detachment	A coach is a partner, but is also separate from the clients and the goals. A certain amount of detachment is positive and appropriate. Coaches who get too involved or wrapped up in what their clients are doing will find it more difficult to be objective and helpful.
Effectiveness	Great coaches value being effective by helping their clients move their goals forward.
Fostering Learning	A learning environment improves self-discovery and awareness. Employees and teams ought to be able to discuss strengths and weaknesses and feel support while developing new skills.
Partnership	Building strong and trusting partnerships is critical in the coaching relationship. Coaching requires trust and open dialogue.
Respect	Each member of the organization adds to its value, including coaches. Work and decisions should demonstrate respect and appreciation for individuals and teams.
Service Oriented	Coaching is a service-oriented activity. The more service oriented you are when coaching, the more likely you are to notice the small details and nuances that will make a difference for your clients.

Table 1-3. The nature of great coaching.

The Focus of Coaching

The client's goals, hopes, and curiosities.

How Coaching Success Is Measured

Coaching is successful when the client is successful in attaining the goals for the coaching. Smaller successes include helping to broaden the client's perspective and develop skills.

The Purposes of Coaching

- Coaching should improve client coachability.
- Coaching should enhance client self-awareness.
- Coaching should uncover potential and build client skills.
- Coaching should help the client get unstuck.
- Coaching should facilitate client breakthroughs.
- Coaching should help create and implement client plans for action.

Important Coaching Skills

- Listen
- Provide feedback
- Ask the right questions
- Relate experiences
- Generate alternatives
- Engender trust
- Facilitate change/transition
- Improve coachability
- Be curious
- Put aside personal agenda
- Be fully present
- Implement coaching practices and tools
- Develop strategies and plans
- Be direct
- Be empathetic
- Be quiet
- Provide encouragement
- Connect information
- Improve motivation for change or action
- Believe in the client's ability
- Be nonjudgmental
- Have humility
- Be self-aware
- Develop theories of motivation
- Increase knowledge of the business
- Contract

Values Important to Coaching

- Acceptance
- Authenticity
- Detachment
- Fostering Learning
- Respect
- Adventure
- Courage
- Effectiveness
- Partnership
- Service Oriented

In the next chapter, you will explore a coaching model.

2

A Coaching Model

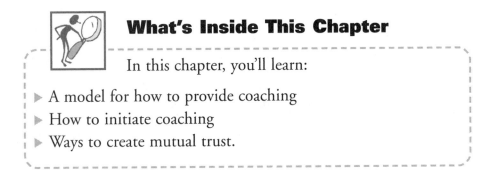

What's Inside This Chapter

In this chapter, you'll learn:

▶ A model for how to provide coaching
▶ How to initiate coaching
▶ Ways to create mutual trust.

In chapter 1, you explored the purposes of coaching and the basic assumptions and beliefs that facilitate effective coaching. In this chapter, the focus is on offering a process for how to coach clients. There are dozens of models for coaching, and no one model is the standard. Coaching is a personal and intimate service, and you will find that most experienced coaches have created their own style and process that they believe works best for their clients. Sometimes the coaching process is so organic and seemingly spontaneous that it is hard to see that there are concrete steps the coach is following. Most coaching models include process steps for engaging the client, contracting, goal setting, assessing, having conversations, developing, and action planning. In figure 2-1, these core steps are assembled into a model for coaching that you can use and personalize.

Figure 2-1. A model for coaching.

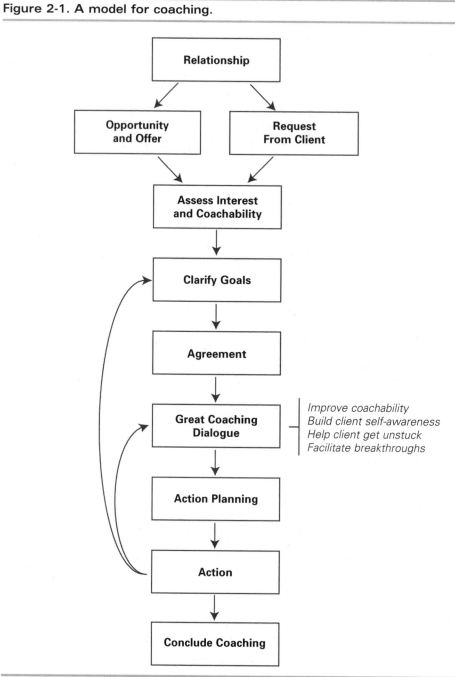

Establish a Relationship With Your Client

One of the most important aspects of coaching is the strength of the relationship between coach and client. Within an organization, a good relationship must precede coaching for it to be most effective. This can present a challenge for managers, trainers, human resources professionals, and organization development practitioners who need to coach people with whom they have not connected. Table 2-1 shows the various elements of a strong coach-client relationship and the actions you can take to build strong and connecting relationships.

Coaching is tough if you do not have strong relationships with your clients. You can speed up the process by having deep and meaningful conversations. If you have been asked to coach someone whom you do not know well, spend some time getting to know each other. Time spent building a foundation to your relationship will be well worth the initial effort and will allow you to understand the client's needs and goals more fully and quickly.

Opportunity and Offer

As a coach, you are tuned to observe people and listen for their goals and challenges. Bob mentions in a meeting that he is working on a big, new project but is struggling

Think About This

In his bestselling book, *Never Eat Alone*, Keith Ferrazzi suggests you "go deep fast." You should move, with lightning speed, past the idle chitchat and get right into topics that mean something. "Transcend the meaningless chitchat about the weather and what company they work for and engage their conversation partners in discussions about stuff that really matters—like their favorite hobbies, their troublesome teenage children, their frustrations at work, their family relationships that really put a strain on them. Only when you talk with someone about their deepest desires and struggles do you get to know and respect and value them as humans, and that's when you really start to bond" (K. Ferrazzi, personal communication). According to Ferrazzi, real connections are intimate. Business relationships are intimate. To be most effective, you need to take more risks and share more of yourself. People judge others, but after getting to know them at a deep level, those early judgments fade away. Connections are personal, they must be, or it is just a superficial association.

Table 2-1. Elements of a strong coach-client relationship.

Element	Description	How to Improve
Mutual Trust	Mutual trust exists when both people feel that they can trust the other and that they will represent each other well. Coaches earn trust by being trustworthy with sensitive information. Fears about the coach being a corporate spy can get in the way of a client's trust in the coach.	Be a role model of trustworthiness in all your dealings. Don't gossip or spread sensitive information about others. Sometimes as a coach, you will need to share your opinions about others, but always do so in a manner that is fair, clear, and respectful. You can build trust quickly by establishing the ground rules up front and then by acting on them consistently.
Shared Purpose	As a coach, you will need to share the desire to help your clients meet their goals. Shared purpose does not mean that you both have the same goals, only that as a coach, you are committed and interested in helping your clients achieve their goals.	Show interest, and reinforce the importance of your clients' goals. Demonstrate that you are engaged and supportive of what they want to accomplish. Make it clear to your clients that your goal is to help them meet their goals. Show respect for the goals that your clients choose. Although you should help your clients shape and clarify goals, you should not try to talk them out of or redirect their goals. By focusing your coaching conversation on their goals, you will show your clients that you are interested in and support their aims.
Intimacy	Connecting relationships are intimate in that they get beyond superficial talk to explore hopes, dreams, fears, and feelings.	Develop intimacy by talking about what matters with your clients. Share yourself, and ask questions that go deep into the topic. Reinforce meaningful conversations and sharing. Quickly move beyond what's on the surface to explore your clients' hopes, dreams, and struggles.
Openness	You and your clients can candidly share thoughts, even those that might be sensitive or embarrassing. This level of dialogue is important to the success of your coaching.	Treat candid thoughts with respect. Do not judge or otherwise make your clients feel as though you are evaluating them. Be candid and forthcoming with information. Ask provocative and evocative questions that facilitate openness.

with how to get it going. Susan says she wishes she could learn how to lead better. You see a manager who seems overwhelmed and frustrated. These are all excellent opportunities for coaching. Once you see the opportunity, you will want to offer help in the form of coaching.

But how do you approach someone? As stated in chapter 1, it is not advisable to say to someone, "Would you like some coaching?" Why? This question might put your potential client on the defensive and generally signals the start of advice. It is better to approach the person sharing your observations and offering assistance. For example:

- ▶ "I heard you mention in the staff meeting that you are struggling with how to best plan and implement your new project. Sometimes we just need to get all our ideas and concerns out and organized. I would be happy to help walk through those conversations with you if you think it might help."
- ▶ "I admire your goal to continue developing your leadership skills. If you would like help creating specific goals and a plan that can fit into your crazy schedule, I would be happy to work with you on that."

Recognizing the opportunity for coaching and offering your services in a non-threatening and open manner is a great way to enroll clients who are coachable and ready to make something great happen.

Request for Coaching

Sometimes clients come directly to you. They have goals and want help reaching them. If they come to you, clients are generally more coachable and engaged. They recognize that coaching might be helpful and are ready to get started. You may need to help clients understand what coaching looks and feels like, but once they understand that the focus is on their goals, they will likely buy into the process.

Basic Rule 5

Using a particular coaching process is not critical, but most processes incorporate the elements of relationship building, contracting, goal setting, having conversations, action planning, and following up.

The exception to this is when potential clients are told to get coaching. This is not an optimal situation because they are more likely to be defensive and uncoachable. If they do not want coaching and are only coming to you because they were told to, the coaching will have little effect. To try to win them over, share the benefits of coaching and ensure them that the coaching sessions will focus on what they deem to be their most important goals. Put their minds at ease that you will not be reporting to their bosses about every conversation.

Noted

Forced coaching is often a waste of time, energy, and resources. Work with senior leaders to ensure people are not forced into coaching.

Assess Interest and Coachability

How interested and engaged are your clients? Are they ready to work on their goals in earnest? Before you determine how long and often you want to meet with your clients, you will want to gauge their interests. If there is an immediate project or goal, you may suggest meeting for a longer period of time or for a short time each day. For long-term goals, meeting weekly, biweekly, or monthly will suffice.

At this point, you also want to observe their behaviors to determine whether they are being coachable. Their coachability will determine whether they will be receptive during the critical initial stages of coaching. If they are not being coachable, you may need to address this before progressing. Chapter 5 offers techniques to determine and improve client coachability.

Clarify Goals

Helping clients clarify their goals is important. Many clients will have only vague notions about their goals. Others will hold on to outdated or unrealistic goals. Some clients will not know what their goals are at all. Some goals will be murky or too broad. You will want to help your clients craft specific goals that they find inspiring and meaningful.

Think About This

Help your client create goals that are both inspiring and actionable. Goals should be neither too broad nor too specific and should be challenging, but not impossible.

- **Too broad and vague**: My goal is to get a promotion (also not inspiring).
  Better: My goal is to develop leadership skills and a reputation of being a great leader, such that I can qualify for a broader role in one year.
- **Too low**: My goal is to complete a week of quality training. (That's not a goal, it's a tactic.)
  Better: My goal is to ensure I get and stay current with what's state-of-the-art in direct marketing techniques, tools, and philosophies.
- **Not realistic**: My goal is to receive a promotion every year for the next three years.
  Better: My goal is to lead my team to being a top contributor and benchmarked by other teams in two years.

Coaching should assist clients in creating visions for success. You will want to help them define what a home run looks like relative to their goals. Together, you should agree about what success will look like and how they will know when it has been achieved. Once the goals are clarified and defined, you should help your clients assess today's reality relative to their goals. Ask them to share how much information they have collected, their current results, and their basic assumptions and beliefs about the goals. The end product of this work is a crisp explanation of your clients' goals, how far they are from achieving them, and an idea of their current approaches.

Gain Agreement

The agreement phase may happen earlier in the coaching process, but it is often not cemented until goal setting is complete. Once the goals are clear, the coaching becomes relevant and more tangible. Your clients may feel a bit tenuous until their goals are articulated and they understand the focus for the coaching. You will want to come to an agreement on the following:

- ▶ the format of coaching sessions
- ▶ the frequency and duration of coaching sessions

- ▶ the purpose and scope of the coaching
- ▶ the ground rules about confidentiality, candor, coachability, and participation.

In addition, coaching conversations will be more effective when you and your client agree on your roles. Each situation might call for slightly different roles based on the size and scope of the work. Table 2-2 offers a starting point for defining roles.

Table 2-2. Coaching roles.

Coach's Role	Client's Role
Encourage your client. Reinforce the interest in the goals.	Share goals, desired outcomes, and hopes.
Help your client define and clarify goals.	Openly discuss frustrations, problems, setbacks, questions, and successes.
Keep discussions on track and moving.	Share relevant information.
Ask stimulating questions.	Discuss assumptions, opinions, and points of view relative to the goals.
Summarize and clarify discussion topics.	Participate in creating and implementing action plans.
Help your client develop an action plan.	Take ownership of asking for coaching and follow up.
Offer resources or tools to improve the client's self-awareness or skills.	Review progress to goals.
Facilitate the client's coachability.	Be open to exploring new ideas and approaches.
Make agreements about the next steps and follow up.	Share setbacks or barriers.
Demonstrate a sincere interest in helping your client achieve goals.	Be highly coachable.

The agreement phase of coaching can be quick and informal or you may choose to formalize your agreements in writing. Do whichever is best for your clients and puts them at ease.

Noted

The agreement phase of coaching is like the contracting phase for consulting.

Great Coaching Dialogue

The coaching conversation begins as you ask questions that expand your clients' thinking. You want to broaden your clients' viewpoints such that they may see new possibilities or attack challenges from a different perspective. When done well, your clients will leave the coaching conversations feeling energized and ready to conquer their goals.

This phase of coaching is where you play the roles of detective, catalyst, and facilitator. Much of this book addresses how to generate excellent coaching conversations that help move your clients forward:

- ▶ Chapter 4: How to Create Great Coaching Dialogue
- ▶ Chapter 5: Coachability
- ▶ Chapter 6: Building Client Self-Awareness
- ▶ Chapter 7: Helping Clients Get Unstuck
- ▶ Chapter 8: Facilitating Breakthroughs.

Each of these invaluable services occurs in conversation and is part of creating an effective coaching practice. Together, you and your clients will want to diagnose approaches that will help them meet their goals. In addition, you will generate inquiry and offer ideas and options that improve forward momentum. Great dialogue will also help clients move past barriers and setbacks.

Action Planning

It can be very satisfying to work with a client to create a robust action plan. When the action plan is complete, there is a sense of relief and clarity because goals are known and the path to achieve the goals is real. Action planning is an important part of coaching because it improves relevance and results. Table 2-3 lists the elements of a great action plan.

Table 2-3. Elements of a great action plan.

Element	Purpose
Brief goals statement	Helps the client communicate goals in a succinct way. Ensures that the action plan items are addressing the goals.
Broad timeline	Focuses the client on when the goals will be achieved.
Actions that improve connectedness	Answers the question, "Who should I know and with whom should I share my goals?" Includes individuals, organizations, publications, and teams.
Actions that get the client in action	Defines the small actions that might make a big difference: emails, personal visits, research, and other tasks that move the goals forward.
Actions that help the client get unstuck	Gets rid of barriers and sources of frustration.
Measurements	Defines how progress will be determined and defined.
Milestones	Breaks down larger goals into smaller components so that progress and success can be acknowledged and celebrated along the way.
Development	Establishes the skills and experiences that will benefit the client and how the development will occur.
Progress	Provides an easy reference for how well things are going and where additional focus and progress is needed.

It is important that you follow up on action items and help your client update and change the plan as needed. A well-crafted action plan can serve as a reference for ongoing coaching conversations and should be incorporated into your client's other schedules and plans.

Helping Your Client Take Action

Once they complete their action plans, your clients will want to get started if they have not already. Although action is listed late in the coaching process, your clients will likely be taking action during all phases of coaching. Being in action is a satisfying way to move goals forward. That said, it is important to ensure that actions are focused and worthwhile. Being in action in the wrong direction will drain your clients of hope and energy, so be careful not to suggest too many actions until the goal-setting process is complete. As figure 2-1 shows, additional goal setting or coaching dialogue follows action or the coaching concludes.

Noted

There are three kinds of actions. Great actions are those that are good ideas. Right actions are those that are good uses of resources and time given other options. Great and right actions are those that are good to do and the best actions in terms of value and efficiency. Very few actions are both great and right. Help your clients choose great and right actions.

Conclude Coaching

Some coaching relationships go on indefinitely, while others are project or goal based. Once your clients successfully implement (or abandon) their action plans, it may be time to conclude the coaching relationship. This does not mean that you will never coach them again; it just means that this coaching project is finished. Sometimes the coaching ends because the goals were achieved. This is a great outcome, and you should celebrate.

Sometimes the coaching ends because your clients lose interest or decide to put off the work. This happens and you should not fight it. If your clients do not want to continue, convincing them to continue coaching meetings will be a waste of everyone's time and energy. You should do everything you can to understand the barriers getting in the way of your clients' progress and help as much as you can.

To conclude the coaching and create closure, ask for a brief meeting to tidy up any loose ends. Take the time to ask for feedback from your clients about what worked well and any improvements to the coaching process that they would recommend. Offer articles or information you had been gathering for future coaching sessions. You never know, one of the articles might inspire them to get re-engaged in coaching. Offer your assistance in the future.

This coaching process will give you a framework from which to begin coaching. Learning a particular coaching process is not critical, although you might find it helpful to use an established process at first. You will notice that these process elements resemble the phases of action planning, a fundamental model used by organization development practitioners. This makes sense because coaching is a change intervention applied to one person or a small group. As with action research, an ongoing coaching relationship includes examining results, defining new actions, and then assessing the results again (research—action—research).

Getting It Done

Helping your clients clarify and articulate their goals is critical. Practice by defining your goals. Use exercise 2-1 as a guide.

Exercise 2-1. Crafting your goals.

Question	Your Response	Consider This
What do you want to accomplish? What accomplishment can you get excited about working toward?		Ensure your goal is not too broad or narrow. Can you clearly articulate your goal in 60 seconds? Share you goal with three other people to test its clarity.
What would a home run look like?		Express one ultimate home run or several milestones.
How will you measure success?		How will you know when you have achieved your goal?
What's the current reality? How far do you need to go?		Be honest about your progress or struggles to date. Doing so will help you get beyond the current reality.
What are the most troublesome barriers and potential opportunities that you will face?		Acknowledge barriers and potential opportunities to help you achieve your goal.

To test how well you defined your goals, share them with three other people. Notice whether the goals are clear or confusing. Express your goals in a fashion that is inspiring by sharing what's special about what you want to accomplish and why these goals are important to you. Sharing your goals is a great way to enroll others in enabling your success. As a coach, you will want to encourage your clients to share their goals with many people.

In the next chapter, you will learn several helpful concepts for coaches.

3

Concepts Important
to Coaching

■ ■

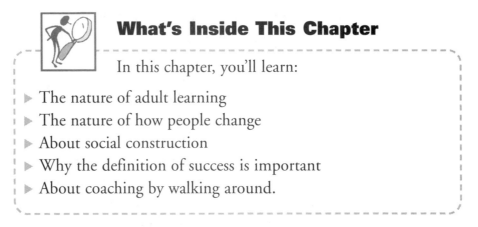

What's Inside This Chapter

In this chapter, you'll learn:

▶ The nature of adult learning
▶ The nature of how people change
▶ About social construction
▶ Why the definition of success is important
▶ About coaching by walking around.

Adult Learning Theory

Coaches help their clients learn, grow, and realize potential. This is not always easy because adult learners can be resistant, fickle, or choosy about the ways and under which conditions they learn. Although it is generally not the coaches providing the training nor the development, you will need to influence your clients' willingness and interests in continuous learning. Here are a few key points about adult learning and how coaches should use this information:

- ▶ Adult learners need to feel the new information and skills directly link to and benefit their goals. Your clients will need to be enrolled with their hearts and minds to be engaged in the learning.

- ▶ Adult learners respond well to real-world examples and applications. Be sure to have conversations with your clients about how the principles and practices relate to their realities.

- ▶ Adult learners resist and repel being forced to attend trainings. They want to come up with the ideas for learning and development on their own or have a list of options from which to choose. Coaches should refrain from prescribing training or development. Instead, have open conversations with your clients and ask questions that allow the clients to discover and determine their development options.

- ▶ Adult learners may be defensive or feel attacked when training or development is recommended to them. Put your clients in the driver's seats, asking them to define their goals and the information or skills that would most help them reach their goals.

- ▶ Adult learners are invested in their careers and successes. They may be reluctant to share their mistakes or weaknesses. Help your clients find the right learning environments and redefine success such that open discussions and learning evoke less fear and insecurity.

- ▶ Adult learners own their progresses and welcome clear feedback along the way. Help your clients determine how well the trainings are progressing, and encourage them to begin applying their new skills right away.

- ▶ Adult learners come to trainings or development sessions with years of previous experiences, opinions, and mindsets. Ensure that your clients have the opportunity to share, acknowledge, and move beyond their biases. Concepts and practices that run counter to their usual ways of being will be accepted and applied slowly. Coaches should understand and allow time for this transition to occur.

- ▶ Adult learners cannot be forced to learn; they must be coachable, and this is their choice. Help facilitate coachability through open and candid conversations focused on the goals they feel passionately about achieving.

Basic Rule 6

Adults learn differently than children, and coaches need to understand the adult learning theory to enable their clients to build skills and realize their potential growths.

Each client will offer you different coaching challenges and opportunities. Some clients will behave like sponges and seek training and development. Others will resist continuing to develop. By listening to what your clients say and do not say about their goals and motivations, you can ask questions that will allow them to self-discover and select appropriate development experiences.

Think About This

When you begin to work with your clients, ask them to share the development experiences they have most enjoyed and those that they did not find enjoyable or helpful. Offer development suggestions that share characteristics (method, length, participation level, timing) with the experiences they most enjoyed.

Change and Transition

To realize maximum benefits, coaching needs to facilitate client change and transition. If the status quo and current practices were working, clients would not be seeking coaching. Coaching, by its very nature, is about facilitating personal transition. In 1991, William Bridges published a book called *Managing Transitions* that addresses how people respond to change. You should not coach clients without considering the process people go through to transition. There are other models of personal transition, but the Bridges Transition Model is the most comprehensive and has stood the test of time.

Change and transition are not the same things, and it is critical that all coaches understand the nature of personal transition. Change is a situation where something transforms. Jobs are added or eliminated. Your clients get promoted or demoted.

The company merges with a competitor. Your clients are asked to take on new projects. New processes are put in place.

Transition is the inner process through which your clients come to terms with changes. Transition is the path they take to react to and get comfortable with changes. The process includes letting go of the way things used to be and getting comfortable with the way things are now. Transition is personal. Each individual will transition at a different speed and in a different manner. When coaching, managing transition means helping clients make this process less painful and troublesome.

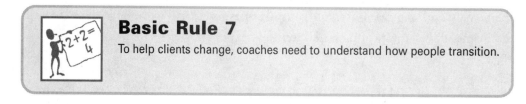

Basic Rule 7

To help clients change, coaches need to understand how people transition.

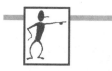

Noted

"Unless transition occurs, change will not work. That's what happens when a great idea falls flat" (Bridges, 1991, p. 4).

Bridges Transition Model

Transition occurs in three phases as shown in figure 3-1: ending, neutral zone, and new beginning.

Phase 1: Ending. Every transition begins with an ending, a loss. When things change, employees leave behind the way things used to be. They are left searching for new ways to define reality. Even if the change is perceived as positive, there is some loss and something that is ending. Before you can transition to the new beginning, you must let go of the way things used to be. Sometimes clients resist giving up ways and practices that have made them successful in the past. They are reluctant to give up what feels comfortable.

Figure 3-1. Bridges Transition Model.

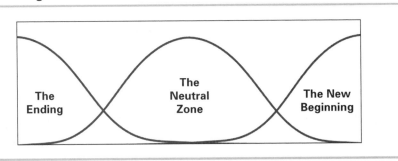

Phase 2: Neutral Zone. The neutral zone is a confusing, in-between state, when clients are on the way to the new beginning. They are no longer in the past, but not yet in the new beginning. It's that ambiguous place in the middle that feels murky. Clients might feel lost. For some, the neutral zone is so full of confusion that getting through it drains their energies. People are driven to get out of the neutral zone; some rush ahead while others retreat into the past. But neither of these approaches is advisable, for the neutral zone has a purpose.

Although the neutral zone can be confusing or even distressing, it can also be a creative place. Time in the neutral zone is not wasted, for this is where the real transformation takes place. The change can continue forward on something close to its own schedule while the transition is being attended to, but if the transition is not dealt with, the change may collapse. Clients cannot do the things the new situations require until they come to grips with what is being asked of them.

Phase 3: New Beginning. The new beginning can only happen after your clients have let go of the past and have spent some time in the neutral zone. In this phase, they accept the reality of the change and start to identify with the new situation.

Some clients fail to get through transition because they do not let go of the old ways and mark the ending; others fail because they become frightened and confused by the neutral zone and don't stay in it long enough. Some, however, do get through these first two phases of transition, but then freeze when they face the third phase. The new beginning requires clients to behave in a new way, and that can be concerning as it tests competence and sense of value. Clients may try to hang back during the final phase of transition if the organization has punished people for mistakes. They will wait to see how others are going to handle the new beginning before jumping in.

Table 3-1 gives a list of behaviors you might see as people transition.

Table 3-1. Behaviors associated with transition.

Phase of Transition	What It Might Look Like
Ending	Avoidance, disbelief, shock, anger, sabotage, carelessness
Neutral Zone	Detachment, withdrawal, confusion, lack of attentiveness, indifference, creativeness, risk taking, experimentation, participation
New Beginning	Behavior consistent with the change, focused on purpose, renewed energy, clarity of role, competence

Facilitating Personal Transition

It is important for coaches to understand and be able to recognize the phases of transition. Your clients' successes will depend on their transitioning well to changes in the organization and in their lives. Often they will not realize they are stuck or struggling with their reactions to the changes. Table 3-2 suggests ways to help your clients transition to changes.

The Bridges Transition Model is an invaluable tool for coaches. By integrating planning for changes and planning for transitions, your coaching will be more robust and successful. Your clients' well-thought-out plans can fail if the clients do not transition fully. Sharing the model and training your clients on transition management will improve their abilities to implement changes within their departments.

Think About This

Although nonstop change is an inevitable reality of today's business climate, you can help your clients deal with many changes. Facilitate conversations where your clients separate the various changes with which they are trying to react. Define what is happening with each change, and help your clients remove the emotion or drama involved, as this will only get in the way of progress. Notice, discuss, and help your clients reduce victim conversations.

Table 3-2. How to facilitate transition.

Phase of Transition	Suggestions to Facilitate Transition
Ending	Help your clients get all the information they need to fully understand the change.
	Clarify what is and is not ending. Help your clients acknowledge what's real and where emotion or exaggeration is getting in the way.
	Help your clients determine ways to mark the ending.
	Help your clients openly acknowledge losses.
Neutral Zone	Help your clients determine what they do and do not know and create temporary practices for dealing with ambiguity.
	Help your clients manage expectations during this time of uncertainty.
	Help your clients come up with ideas for training and skill development to meet the needs of the new change.
	Encourage experimentation and brainstorming of ideas.
New Beginning	Encourage open conversations about setbacks and challenges and enlist your clients to be part of the solution.
	Help your clients celebrate successes, even small ones.

Social Construction of Reality

"When people talk to one another, the world gets constructed" (Burr, 1995, p. 7). Social constructionists believe that reality is socially constructed. What does this mean? When people talk about something, they define it and make it real. It is during daily interactions that people construct their versions of knowledge and what they believe is real. Two different languages or conversations can create two realities. Your conversations, your talk, make things real to you. The word *conversation* is used broadly here to include verbal exchanges, written communications, nonverbal communications, and various other media forms. One million people reading a story in the newspaper can create new conversations that shift reality for themselves. In Alaska, the Eskimos have 11 different words for various types of snow. They experience 11 different realities about snow. Most people only have three or four ways to define snow. When a crime is committed in a neighborhood, several conversations and several realities exist—those of the police, the criminal, the neighbors, and the witnesses.

As a theory and practice, social constructionism can be helpful to coaches. When your clients are open to the fact that reality is created in conversation, they will more easily notice and modify assumptions that are not helpful. According to Burr (1995) in *An Introduction to Social Constructionism:*

> Social constructionism insists that we take a critical stance toward our taken-for-granted ways of understanding the world (including ourselves). It invites us to be critical of the idea that our observations of the world unproblematically yield its nature to us, to challenge the view that conventional knowledge is based on objective, unbiased observation of the world. (p. 7)

Don't confuse what you see as reality with objective truth. In many situations, particularly those dealing with people, there is no one correct way to view the situation. Perceptions about reality are important to coaches and determine clients' behaviors and results. For years, the prevailing conversation was that the world was flat. During this time, of course, the world was round, but people's actions and behaviors reflected a reality that the world was flat. It is important to know what your clients believe is real. Is the situation hopeless? Are people conspiring to make them fail? Was the decision dead wrong? These are all views of what's going on in the workplace, and they are socially constructed.

To change what's real, change the conversation. One of the most powerful ways to create change is to shift what people are talking about. Notice what your clients are talking about. Are the conversations in support of the change they seek? Often, they are not.

Think About This

It is important that you know about the social construction of reality, but your clients may not respond well to being tutored on the theory. Help clients determine which conversations are helpful and those that are getting in the way of their successes. Help your clients ensure they are creating the reality that is most helpful.

Victim conversations are a good example of conversations that define a reality that is unhelpful. It might be a struggle to get your clients to experiment taking on an alternative conversation and reality, but once they do, they will see the benefits.

Definition of Success

You spend much of your waking hours in conversation with yourself. Your mind is continuously processing your internal dialogue, or self-talk. This chatter covers hopes, fears, assumptions, opinions, accomplishments, conclusions, stories, and questions. At the core of your self-talk are your beliefs about what it means to be successful, or your definition of success. Your definition of success determines how you assess accomplishment and failure. Your definition of success is potent because it shapes the choices you make and the way in which you approach your work and life.

You may find that your clients are getting stuck or stalled because of the way they define success. For example, managers might define success as being in charge and being right. (They won't word it this way, but this is very common.) This definition of success can get in the way of being responsive to candid feedback and input and hamper coachability. Helping clients change their definitions of success to better support their goals is an effective way to help them get moving forward again. When your clients observe and realign their beliefs about success, they set many positive changes in motion because their new beliefs will lead to better actions.

Noted

A definition of success is a set of beliefs about what success looks and feels like. These beliefs may or may not serve your clients' goals or facilitate their successes.

How do you determine your clients' definitions of success? It is not always easy. You cannot ask about their beliefs of success and expect to get a complete answer. This is particularly the case when it comes to darker, or less helpful, beliefs. For example, the belief that being right is important for success is very common. It is unlikely, however, that if you ask your clients about their beliefs of success that they will say they believe being successful means being right.

The most effective way to determine your clients' definitions of success is by asking them questions and observing their behaviors. For example, if your clients are defensive when people bring up ideas in a group setting, they likely believe that being corrected or challenged in front of others is bad. Table 3-3 lists several common, unhelpful beliefs; the behaviors you might observe; and the questions you can ask.

Table 3-3. Unhelpful beliefs that make up a definition of success.

Common Belief About Success	Observable Behaviors	Questions to Ask
I need to be right.	Defensive, uncoachable, not inclusive, sticks to initial ideas, delays communicating, hides mistakes	How do you feel when people challenge your ideas in front of others? Do you think your manager judges you based on whether your ideas are right or wrong? When was the last time you asked your team to share their ideas with you?
I need to look good.	Defensive in a group setting, makes excuses, casts blame toward others, delays communicating, hides mistakes	When something goes wrong, do you feel the need to find out who is to blame? Why? When was the last time you admitted a mistake to your manager or staff?
I need to be in charge.	Disempowers, takes over in meetings, makes decisions without asking for or considering input	At your staff meetings, what percentage of the time do you speak? What's your role in meetings? Who attends project update meetings? Do you find it difficult to let go of control? Why?
I can't trust anyone except myself.	Fails to delegate, micromanages	Do you delegate tasks or tasks and ownership? Would you describe yourself as a hands-on manager? Do you believe that in order for something to be done right, you need to do it?
I need to be ready before I move forward.	Inaction, paralysis by analysis, asks for too much development or coaching before beginning to move forward	Why has this project not moved forward? How much research do you feel is necessary before you can move on? Do you worry about making mistakes?
Things will get better soon.	Inaction, excuses for not moving forward, abdicates ownership	Are you waiting for things to calm down before acting? What do you think is going to happen in the next year that will affect this project? Why do you think this is not the right time?

Did you notice that many of these unhelpful beliefs have a common theme of needing control? A need for control often gets in the way of goal attainment because most goals are best accomplished with the input and cooperation of others. The other theme that is common is making excuses to justify inaction. These are not always bad beliefs to hold. For example, in an emergency situation, it might be important to take charge and be in control. You may find that your clients have other beliefs that are getting in the way of progress. By asking thoughtful questions and observing how your clients react to others, you can get a good idea of the key elements of their definitions of success. If your clients are open and willing, suggest that they create ideal definitions of success that will best serve their goals. A good definition of success reduces negative drama and self-criticism. Here are several beliefs that are useful in a business setting:

- I am successful when I get diverse input and consider opposing views because doing so will strengthen my plan and allow me to consider potential barriers to implementation.
- I am successful when I am highly coachable because I get more and better input with which to make decisions.
- People will offer me more and better ideas when I accept feedback positively and with appreciation.
- I will be seen as successful when I get the job done while building and maintaining relationships.
- I will enjoy more cooperation and assistance if I am a pleasure to work with.
- I will enjoy more success when I am assertive and strong when needed most, and flexible and accommodating when possible.
- Success means producing results and keeping my promises.
- It is better to have the best end product even if this means admitting I was wrong or changing the path. Being stubborn and unwilling to change gets in the way of my success.

Determining your clients' definitions of success will help you evaluate the barriers getting in the way and make helpful suggestions. If your clients adopt healthy and beneficial definitions of success, they will find their work more fruitful and satisfying.

Coaching by Walking Around

Coaches internal to an organization can provide a valuable and fast-acting service: coaching by walking around (CBWA). When CBWA regularly, you are able to

Think About This

What's your definition of success? How do you define successful coaching? Some coaches are less effective because they define success as being brilliant or offering their clients great ideas. As stressed in chapter 1, coaching is a service-oriented activity and the focus is on the client. Take a few moments to assess your definition of success and determine if it is serving your goal to be a great coach.

observe and assist with situations in real time. A practice of CBWA is a great way to increase your value and effect within the organization. Here are some characteristics of CBWA:

- Visits are ad hoc and unplanned.
- The intent is to check in with people, not minister advice.
- Visits are not so frequent or lengthy that you become a distraction or nuisance.
- CBWA allows you to observe the tenor of the culture and how the organization is performing.

Basic Rule 8

CBWA means "coaching by walking around" and is a great way for coaches to assist with ad hoc or short-term challenges.

When CBWA, you increase your visibility and accessibility. CBWA also ensures that you are in tune with what is really going on in the workplace. It is also a great way to find new clients for ongoing coaching because you build more and stronger relationships. Here's how CBWA works:

- Get up from your desk and walk around the operation. Be interested (not in a monitoring way) in what people are doing. If you work for a large organization, select different parts of the organization to visit each day.
- Check in with a few people as you stroll through the workplace. Pick up on nonverbal clues that will tell you who is too busy to chat and those who might welcome a conversation. Respect people's time and never loiter.

- Ask open-ended questions about how projects or programs are going. Offer to be a sounding board and help the people process their thinking. If they say yes, ask them if they want to do this now or at another time. If they decline, cheerfully offer help in the future.
- CBWA can be performed before meetings by showing up five minutes early and checking in with the first people to arrive.
- CBWA can be performed in the lunchroom by joining different groups of people each day and getting to know them better.

It is important that you understand the altruistic nature of CBWA and that this comes across as you stroll the operations. Coaches who are more visible and available will naturally become involved and able to assist with more situations. CBWA is also a great way to begin small-group coaching.

Think About This

You can add a lot of value to the organization by providing ad hoc coaching, but you have to be accessible. Most ad hoc coaching conversations occur spontaneously and because they are convenient. If you load your schedule with too many meetings and projects, you will not be able to provide quality coaching services. Get up and walk around several times a day to check in with clients and ask for input on your projects.

Getting It Done

Notice the informal conversations in your workplace. What do they tell you about how people feel about their jobs and the company? Share your observations with your human resources department and together brainstorm the conversations that would support a better work experience and methods for sharing these beneficial conversations.

Try CBWA three times per week for one month. Each week, reflect on the path you took and the conversations that occurred. Adjust your approach where needed to improve the amount and quality of connections you make.

In the next chapter, you will explore ways to create dynamic coaching dialogue.

4

How to Create Great Coaching Dialogue

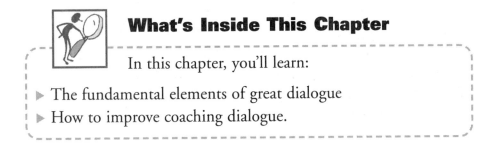

What's Inside This Chapter

In this chapter, you'll learn:

▶ The fundamental elements of great dialogue
▶ How to improve coaching dialogue.

The conversation is exciting, fast paced, and intellectually stimulating. Everyone is smart and focused. People solve problems quickly and think on their feet. Do you wish you could experience a work environment this provocative? Some work-places are like this and, more often than not, the reason is that they hire the right people and foster productive and engaging dialogue. People are talking about topics that matter and what they talk about matters to them.

Painters need to understand the nature and properties of oils and canvas. English teachers need to know semicolons and dangling participles. Coaching occurs in conversation, and so coaches need to be master conversationalists. As a coach, you have the opportunity to create great dialogue and help your clients become master conversationalists. When your work improves the level of dialogue, your effect on the organization will go beyond the help you offer your clients.

Basic Rule 9

Coaching occurs in conversation, and coaches need to become masters of creating great dialogue.

Noted

"Language is an essential part of coaching and, in fact, it could be said that the essential job of the coach is to provide a new language for the client" (Flaherty, 1999, p. 28).

You know great dialogue when you experience it. The level of engagement and energy far outshines the average business talk. Participants are actively thinking, listening, and contributing. Figure 4-1 shows the elements of great dialogue, and they are discussed below in more detail.

Relevance: The topic of discussion is one that people care about and makes a difference to their lives.

Inquiry: Questions are being asked that move the topic forward. Questions are both provocative and evocative.

Freedom: Participants feel free to share their ideas and thoughts, even those on the fringe. The conversation is open.

Connectedness: There is a sense of shared purpose or interest. The participants feel connected to one another. All or most of the participants are contributing.

Reception: Participants listen well, interpret the information, provide feedback, and reinforce contribution.

Empowerment: People feel as though they have some influence on the topic being discussed. This would ideally mean they can move the problem or opportunity forward, but could also mean they can move the intellectual debate further.

Play: The conversation is fun and full of energy. The dialogue has an energy to it that flows and can be playful.

Great dialogue will have many or all of these characteristics. A work environment where people engage in lively dialogue will quickly solve problems and be

Figure 4-1. Elements of great dialogue.

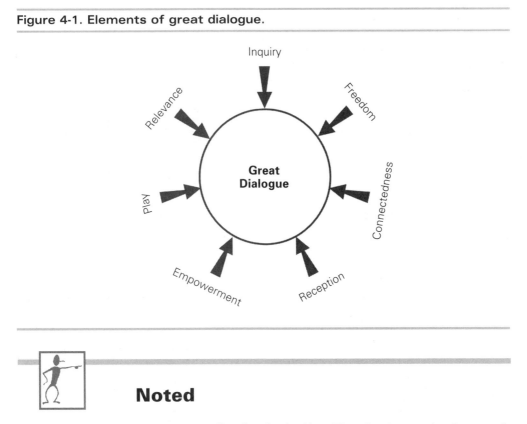

Noted

"The coach's question proposes a direction for looking. The client's attention is naturally drawn in that direction. With each new question, the coach encourages additional looking along a path—or shifts the path, allowing the curiosity to steer the looking" (Whitworth, Kimsey-House, and Sandahl, 1998, p. 66).

---

better able to seize opportunities. As a coach, you can help create an environment that encourages effective dialogue by addressing each one of these characteristics.

Ensuring Dialogue Relevance

When you work with your clients, you will want to focus on their goals and their most troublesome barriers. If your clients do not seem engaged, then maybe the topic is not relevant enough or you are not approaching it in a way that is appealing to them. You might need to bring up topics the clients would prefer to avoid. If you ask the right provocative or evocative questions, you should be able to grab their interests.

Think About This

If your clients do not think that your coaching conversations are relevant, this is a problem. Have open conversations about how they would like to see the meetings change. Try to accommodate their hopes while giving them what they need to get unstuck (not always the same things).

Creating Excellent Inquiry

Inquiry is at the core of coaching. Clients seek coaching because they want to explore and improve their effectiveness and learn more about themselves. Asking questions is a great way to jumpstart inquiry. There are several types of questions, and they are not all treated equally. The two most common types of questions are closed-ended and open-ended:

- ▶ Closed-ended questions: Ask for a short or one-word answer. "Do you want to be successful?"
- ▶ Open-ended questions: Ask for a longer, individualized answer. "What would you like to accomplish this year?"

To create effective inquiry, you need to look deeper than whether the question is closed- or open-ended. Both types can be poor or excellent questions, although open-ended questions involve the client more. The two examples listed above are both poor questions. They are not interesting and are much too general.

There is another way to look at creating inquiry that focuses on the quality of the questions you ask. As a coach, you want to make sure that your questions are either provocative or evocative:

- ▶ Provocative questions: Excite and stimulate conversation. "What would happen if...?"
- ▶ Evocative questions: Pull in participants, and help bring things to mind. "What kind of work makes you feel most engaged and satisfied?"

Inquiry plays a significant role in coaching. Select questions that move the topic forward and engage your client.

Noted

Provocative questions are interesting and intriguing. Evocative questions grab your clients such that they can see themselves in the dialogue. (Evoke means to pull in.)

Socrates, a Greek philosopher, was well known for his provocative and evocative questions. Using Socratic questions can generate rich information that helps your clients succeed. You can help your clients develop critical thinking and creativity skills. Socratic questions enable coaches to create an intriguing and fruitful dialogue. The Socratic method emphasizes the use of thought-provoking questions to promote learning (instead of offering opinions and advice). A well-executed Socratic question stretches the mind and challenges widely held beliefs.

When it comes to coaching, the more questions you ask, the better. But they need to be great questions. If you are comfortable sharing your opinions and ideas, your challenge will be to resist giving advice. Advice rarely improves inquiry. Advice

Noted

Socrates (469–399 B.C.) was a fifth-century Athenian philosopher known for his interactive methods of teaching, examination of the concept of piety, adherence to civil obedience, and inquiries into the basis of virtue. He is best remembered for his ultimate act of civil obedience, administering his own death sentence by drinking hemlock after having been convicted of corrupting the youth of Athens and undermining religion. The approach to philosophy espoused by Socrates was based upon four pillars: ironic modesty, questioning of habit, devotion to truth, and dispassionate reason. The dialogues for which he is so well known had as their goal the understanding and attainment of virtue, which is defined as excellence, skill, or artistry. To that end, Socrates taught by engaging his students in dialogue and questioning widely held beliefs and doctrines. He believed that it was necessary to acknowledge ignorance to take the first step toward genuine knowledge. In defense of the actions that brought upon him a sentence of death, Socrates uttered the timeless assertion, "The unexamined life is not worth living."

may be helpful at times, but the most effective coaching will facilitate your clients' thinking processes. To do this, try using Socratic questions.

Socratic questions are probing, and most are open-ended. You can use these questions in any situation. Inquiry creates change and is the cornerstone of coaching because it helps clients think and solve problems creatively. Socratic questions will also help your clients clarify what they understand and in which areas they need more information. Throughout your coaching session, these questions will bring to light new strategies and ideas. When you ask great questions, you create exciting dialogues that your clients will find intrinsically motivating. Table 4-1 offers a list of Socratic questions.

Using Socratic questions to generate inquiry improves your ability to remain objective by facilitating your clients' self-discoveries. The questions also serve to expand the clients' analyses of the situations and increase the number and quality of possibilities they consider. Using Socratic questions increases the energy of the dialogue and improves your clients' learning.

Table 4-1. Socratic questions.

Situation	Socratic Questions
To clarify your clients' goals	How would you like the change to occur? Why do you want this change? What will things look like in a year if everything goes as planned? What are the consequences of not changing?
To clarify your clients' intents or motives	Why do you want this outcome? How will you benefit? Why is this change important? What gave you this idea? Who will benefit from this change?
To ensure your clients' goals are aligned for success	How does this help you achieve your goal? What does this mean to you? What do you already know about this approach? How does this change affect the other aspects of the organization?
To uncover your clients' basic assumptions	What other assumptions could also be valid? Why do you believe this change is needed? What does your peer/manager/team think about this situation? What would happen if...? Why do you think I asked you this question?
To discover if your clients have enough information	What generalizations have you made? How do you know that ... ? Why is this situation occurring? Have you seen a situation similar to this before? What verification is there to support your claim?
To help your clients see other points of view	What are the pros and cons of your approach? How is this similar to or different from the way you have approached this in the past? What would an opponent of the idea say? What would your customers say? How would your competitors approach this?

Basic Rule 10

A coach should spend much more time listening and asking great questions than offering advice or solutions.

Encouraging the Freedom to Participate Fully

The effectiveness of your coaching can be crippled if you and your clients do not feel comfortable about being open and candid with each other. When you contract with your clients, you will want to agree on how you will handle confidential or sensitive topics. Once you have an agreement, sticking to that agreement will build mutual trust and openness.

In a small-group coaching situation, you will want to establish ground rules and manage participation so everyone is heard and all topics are considered. You may need to be the one to bring up a sensitive topic first to help break the ice for the rest of the group. Ensure that you diplomatically deal with over-participators or comments that squash the group's creativity and engagement.

Think About This

Clients may not make it easy for you to coach instead of giving advice, as they often ask for your opinion. You need to assess whether giving an opinion will be most helpful or if asking a few questions will better service your clients. Though it is not the end of the world to offer a suggestion or to say what you would do, it is often better to engage your clients in a dialogue whereby they discover new possibilities. You might compromise by saying, "I will tell you what I think, but first I'd like to hear why you believe this situation has escalated."

Ensuring Connectedness

Coaches walk a fine line between being involved and objective and being separated. It is better to not get too directly involved in the situations that your clients are working through. Even so, you can be very connected to your clients in that you take ownership of enabling their effectiveness through your coaching. Show an interest in the progress; show them that their successes matter to you. Being connected means having a strong and deep relationship. As a coach, you want to be connected in a way that recognizes and honors the roles you have agreed to as coach and client.

Improving Dialogue Reception

Many things get in the way of dialogue reception. Miscommunication, censored feedback, and poor listening can wreck a conversation. You may not hear what your clients are trying to tell you even if you hear the words they are speaking. Communication between two people goes through each person's filters. Figure 4-2 shows how messages change as they pass through the filters (mindset, biases, and opinions) of both the sender and the receiver.

Figure 4-2. Our communication filters.

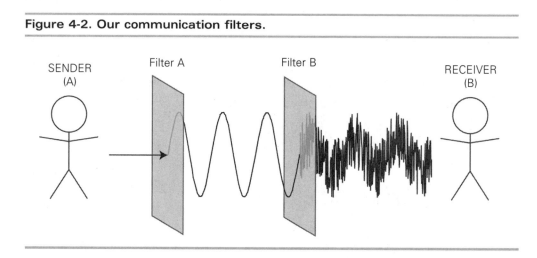

Coaches need to listen to the words that are being said and hear the clients' intentions, or disconnects will occur. Even with the best of intentions, messages can become distorted and confused. Coaches who learn to listen well and provide effective feedback will improve overall dialogue reception.

Active Listening

Active and deep listening is a critical skill for coaches. As mentioned in chapter 1, experienced coaches rated listening as the most important coaching skill. Active listening is critical because so much of your coaching work depends on clear communications and good relationships. It is a way of listening and responding to your clients that improves mutual understanding. Many people are poor listeners. They get distracted, talk too much, and think about what they are going to say next when they should be listening. They assume they know what other people are going to say and tune them out. It can be difficult to take the time and energy to listen actively, but the rewards are worth the effort. You are listening actively when you

- demonstrate a sincere desire to pay attention to the other person (instead of mentally practicing what you are going to say next)
- commit to being coachable and open with the information being received from the other person
- relate to the other person's perspective, and empathize
- seek to understand the other person
- pay attention, and resist being distracted by other things in the environment
- ensure you have interpreted the message as intended through feedback, confirming, restating, or paraphrasing
- reflect on what the other person is saying
- synthesize the information, emotion, and feelings to improve understanding
- clarify the information by asking questions and probing
- validate perceptions and assumptions
- allow the other person to talk
- focus on the other person, and be fully present.

Noted

Active listening is the practice of showing clients that you are listening and interested in what they have to say. This involves giving them your full attention through verbal and nonverbal encouragement and validation.

Many people let full calendars, long to-do lists, stress, and their natural behavioral tendencies get in the way of the ability to actively listen. To get in the habit of listening actively, try these tips:

- Be with the other person, fully present and focused.
- Give the other person good eye contact; don't let your eyes roam around the room.

- Take some notes, but don't look at other papers or reports. Don't take such detailed notes that you are missing the overall message.
- Let the other person talk, and do not worry about filling the lulls between sentences.
- Ask clarifying questions.
- Mentally put yourself in the other person's shoes.
- Respond to what the other person is saying.
- Eliminate distractions like phone, pager, and email pings.

Active listening is a habit that you can and must develop. Being great listeners benefits coaches by reducing misunderstandings, improving information accuracy, and ensuring that they have complete information from which to work. Clients open up more to people who listen well.

Think About This

To test and develop your active listening skills, ask only questions and let other people do most of the talking for one week. Leave 15 seconds between other people's words and your next comment. Focus on the conversation and intently listen to the other people. Pretend you are fascinated with what they are saying, and imagine that their words hold the key to an intriguing puzzle. Guess what? They do!

Giving Effective Feedback

Coaches need to provide clear and candid feedback to help their clients recognize and understand their behaviors. Feedback should be provided with your clients' preferences and coachability triggers in mind. In other words, you need to determine how to best offer feedback in a manner that will be well received and understood by your clients. Here are a few suggestions for providing effective feedback:

- Offer feedback regularly, both positive and negative. Your clients should become accustomed to regular feedback.
- Focus on the behavioral issues that are important and that your clients can do something about. Everyone has many areas to improve. Do not dilute

your feedback by sending too many messages. Focus on the one or two areas that will make the greatest differences to your clients' successes.

▶ Select times and places that are appropriate and conducive to good reception from your clients. Are your clients ready to hear feedback? Clients need to be coachable to make use of feedback.

▶ Let your clients know the purpose of the feedback and how it relates to their goals.

▶ Feedback should be specific and clear. Provide concrete examples about how your clients' behaviors affected others.

▶ Encourage your clients to offer responses to your feedback. Help them process what you have said, and ensure that they heard what you intended to communicate. If they need some time to process what you have said, this is fine.

▶ Follow up without redelivering the feedback. Coaches can become annoying if they repeat the same feedback again and again. You can follow up by helping your clients incorporate any development needs into their action plans. Offer your clients provocative or evocative articles or blog posts that relate to the topic of the feedback (whether reinforcing positive behaviors or addressing negative behaviors).

As a coach, you will need to deliver feedback that might be difficult for your clients to hear. Building positive and trusting relationships and regularly sharing positive feedback will help your clients accept the tough messages more constructively.

Improving Topic Empowerment

Conversations achieve topic empowerment when your clients feel they can have an effect on the discussion and outcome. The topic is within their spheres of influence. When coaching conversations focus on the goals or development areas that are most important to your clients, achieving topic empowerment is not a problem. If your clients do not feel as though they can influence their own goals, then they have defined poor goals. Sometimes clients will not see the full breadth of the influence they have, and you may need to help them broaden their perceptions.

Keeping Conversations Playful

You can do a lot of things that will keep your coaching dialogue playful. A playful conversation does not need to lack seriousness. In this context, playfulness means playing with ideas, concepts, and information such that the conversation's energy level is high. Here are several ways you can improve conversation playfulness:

▶ Ask your client to read interesting and provocative articles prior to your meeting.

▶ Change the context of the meeting to a place that is intellectually stimulating.

▶ Mindmap the conversation.

▶ Share a success story of someone with a similar goal.

▶ Use idea-generation techniques.

▶ Plan the agenda of the coaching meeting so the meeting moves quickly and flows well. Ensure there is an attention grabber at the beginning, and try to plan for a high point to occur toward the end of the meeting.

▶ Make homework assignments that are unconventional and intriguing. For example, ask your clients to contact their favorite role models. Suggest that your clients change one behavior for one week. Suggest a thought-provoking movie or live performance.

Noted

"Curiosity is especially important in coaching because it gets at sources of information that bypass the head. Asking questions for data will yield analysis, reasons, rationale, and explanation. Asking questions out of curiosity will yield deeper—often more genuine—information about feelings and motivation. Information revealed through curiosity is less censored, less carefully crafted, and messier. It will be more real" (Whitworth, Kimsey-House, and Sandahl, 1998, p. 67).

To make conversations more playful, you want to have a variety of contexts and types of information coming together. Tap into the interests and needs of your clients and offer information that will stretch and broaden their perspectives.

Coaching is more of an art than a science. It is a dialogue that you drive and keep focused on the clients. Effective coaching produces energy. Whether your clients leave with more energy and excitement depends on the quality of the dialogue. Great dialogue is stimulating, intriguing, and enlightening; and the best coaches make this happen in a seamless and almost magical way.

Think About This

One of the easiest and most interesting ways you can expose your client to a variety of perspectives is to share posts from Weblogs (blogs). Bloggers cover various aspects of business. Find a few good bloggers who write about topics related to your client's goals. At the end of each coaching session, hand your client three or four blog posts to read before the next meeting. Blog posts offer fresh thinking and new ideas. They are quick and enjoyable to read and may offer your client inspiration or ideas.

Noted

Many facilitation techniques can be applied to one-on-one coaching conversations, including brainstorming, generating ideas, mindmapping, flipcharting, and meeting planning tools.

Basic Rule 11

Coaching is an art because it is expressive, creative, and subjective. Although there are methods and practices that build general techniques (like in art), the best coaches have learned how to transcend protocol and create an environment where amazing things are possible.

Getting It Done

Begin recognizing great and poor dialogue. Use exercise 4-1 to assess the elements of great dialogue that are missing or inadequate and create ideas of ways you can improve the conversation.

Exercise 4-1. Worksheet for diagnosing dialogue elements.

Element of Great Dialogue	Good	Needs Improvement	Possible Action Steps
Relevance			
Inquiry			
Freedom			
Connectedness			
Reception			
Empowerment			
Play			

In the next chapter, you will learn techniques for facilitating your client's coachability.

5

Coachability

What's Inside This Chapter

In this chapter, you'll learn:

▶ What coachability looks like
▶ Techniques for improving client coachability
▶ Pitfalls to avoid that get in the way of client coachability
▶ How your coachability affects your ability to provide great coaching.

Coaching Should Improve Client Coachability

To succeed at reaching their goals, clients will need to be highly coachable. What does being coachable mean? Look at coachability from the perspective of a manager. Much of a manager's day involves guiding others, solving problems, and partnering with peers. It is just as important for managers to get coaching that helps them meet their goals. To benefit from coaching, managers need to be coachable. Coachability is the degree to which they are open to what the environment can offer or the extent to which they accept and consider input and ideas.

Managers' successes depend on whether they are highly coachable when it counts most. Although everyone is coachable some of the time and uncoachable at other times, the most effective managers will be more coachable overall and, most important, during the times when it can make the greatest difference.

Think About This

Begin noticing what coachability and uncoachability look like. Observe how you react to others and how they react to you. Is there an invisible brick wall between you? Why is the wall there? Notice how personality, time of day, and topic affect coachability. In meetings, observe what the meeting leader does that helps or hinders the coachability of the attendees.

You measure coachability by how well your clients interact with the environment; therefore, it is an observable behavior. Coachability is easy to recognize. Table 5-1 shows signs that suggest whether someone is coachable or uncoachable.

When managers are coachable, there is an open, curious, and relaxed quality to their demeanors. Being coachable goes hand-in-hand with confidence and an ownership for results. Coachable managers display a sense of calm and a focus that allows them to take ideas and process them without feeling the need to defend or rationalize current methods. Highly coachable managers see coaching as a tool to produce better results.

By observing how clients behave during meetings and work sessions, you will notice the behavioral cues that signal whether they are coachable. Along with helping your clients improve coachability, you should endeavor to improve your coachability. Recognizing when you are being uncoachable is an important step toward improving your ability to grow and be successful.

Coachability is not a condition, like being pregnant; it is a state of mind. People are not inherently coachable or uncoachable. People have moments during which they are coachable and others during which they are not. Saying that someone is not coachable unfairly classifies that person and does not recognize that coachability is a way of being that can be chosen at any given moment.

Table 5-1. What coachability looks like.

Coachable	Uncoachable
Is not defensive when offered an alternative point of view	Staunchly defends current decisions, practices, and ideas
Welcomes ideas and feedback about ways to improve	Does not listen to suggestions offered by others
	Appears nonreceptive or not interested in coaching
Asks for coaching	Does not use the ideas that others offer; may be dismissive of others
Reflects on and uses ideas that others offer	
Looks for development opportunities, whether in the form of reading, classes, new assignments, or coaching from others	Does not seek self-development nor engage in conversations about self-development
Is open to acknowledging strengths and weaknesses	Believes that asking for input is a sign of weakness; is uncomfortable acknowledging and discussing weaknesses
Handles failures and setbacks with grace and honesty	Is defensive and looks for someone to blame; may hide mistakes rather than openly discuss them
Has confidence and an ownership for results	Is driven to be right

Noted

Coachability is a state of mind that can be changed in an instant.

Improving Client Coachability

When your clients are being uncoachable, trying to coach them can be a waste of time. One of the greatest services a coach can provide clients is to help them be more coachable. To do this you need to have open conversations about coachability, including the things, times, or people that trigger it. By understanding personal triggers, you help the client acknowledge the costs of uncoachability and choose a more productive mindset. Everyone is different, but here are a few examples of uncoachability triggers:

▶ Joan became uncoachable when someone questioned her decisions or opinions in front of her manager or peers. She had a strong need to be right and did not like to be challenged in front of others. Actually, she did not like to be challenged at all.

▸ Kevin did not like to hear ideas or suggestions that affected his tidy existence. He took great pride in planning his time and work. When an idea had the potential to turn his world upside down, even if for the better, he resisted it, regardless of its merit or potential.

▸ Jeremy was uncoachable when overwhelmed with too many tasks. His peers and managers eventually learned that it was best to save ideas and input for when Jeremy was not feeling overwhelmed. Unfortunately, he was overwhelmed a lot.

▸ Cathy was a functional snob. She was coachable when talking with other professionals in her field of expertise, but quickly became defensive and uncoachable when individuals outside her profession offered suggestions.

▸ Lisa's triggers were time based. Lisa was coachable in the morning, but she was less receptive after 3 p.m. Her staff learned to catch her first thing in the morning to receive the best response to their ideas.

Basic Rule 12

Your clients' levels of coachability are of paramount importance. If your clients are being uncoachable, you should help them acknowledge this and become more coachable.

One purpose of coaching is to improve coachability. In fact, if clients are being uncoachable, your sole focus should be on helping them be more coachable. Here are several techniques to improve coachability:

▸ Communicate in ways and using vehicles that appeal to your clients. Do they prefer direct one-on-one communication, or are they more receptive to hearing stories and examples?

▸ Use learning techniques and methods that best suit your clients' styles and behavioral tendencies.

▸ Talk about coachability as a catalyst for success. Clients who believe that being coachable is important to achieving their goals will be more aware of their triggers and more open to coaching.

▸ Ask your clients if they would prefer to reschedule when you notice that they are being uncoachable. Share that they seem distracted or deep in thought and you'd be happy to come back another time.

▸ Talk openly about triggers. Suggest that clients notice when they feel a wall of resistance, and then pause, take a deep breath, and decide to let go of the feelings and be more open.

▸ Ask open-ended questions that get the clients talking about what is on their minds. Tie your conversations to what is important to them.

▸ Ask follow-up questions that enable uncoachable clients to better understand the ideas and suggestions being offered during the meeting.

▸ Be open about the triggers you see. Share techniques you use to be more coachable.

▸ Schedule coaching conversations at times and in an environment that encourages coachability.

It is critical that you are open with your clients about how coachability affects goal attainment. This might be the most important coaching you provide your clients. It helps to understand how your clients are feeling. Table 5-2 offers feelings associated with coachability (left side) and those more common with people who are uncoachable (right side). Notice that feelings on both sides of the chart are common. Remember that people are both coachable and uncoachable every day, and it is normal to seek conversation and input sometimes and not welcome it at other times.

It helps to be open and generous with personal examples. The goal is not to be coachable all the time, as this is unrealistic. It is important to strive to be coachable when it matters most. When you coach, you want to create a climate that puts your clients at ease and makes them open to exploring ideas. The coaching environment can have a significant influence on your clients' levels of coachability.

If your clients are being uncoachable, these techniques could help. Some clients will not respond to your efforts and will remain uncoachable. This is a frustrating situation for coaches, because they want to help, but their clients are not in the mood to be helped. What do you do in this situation? Experienced coaches were asked the following questions: "Is it worth your time to coach someone who is not receptive to coaching (being uncoachable)? How do you handle these situations?" Of the coaches who took part in the survey, 76 percent of them said it is not worth

Table 5-2. Coachable and uncoachable feelings.

Coachable	Uncoachable
Welcomes contrary ideas	Is on the defensive
Is interested in new ideas or perspectives	Does not want any new ideas right now
Is in the mood for coaching	Is not in the mood for coaching
Loves to incorporate changes	Does not want to change plans
Likes some additional training, knowledge, or development	Knows what needs to be done to reach the goal
Likes to talk about weaknesses	Would rather not talk about weaknesses
Feels able to overcome setbacks	Perceives failure as difficult to overcome
Likes to discuss goals	Likes to think about the goal alone before discussing it

Think About This

One way to improve your clients' levels of coachability is to role model coachability. This has an added benefit of helping you achieve your goals. Acknowledge and manage your moments of uncoachability. Use self-talk and other breakthrough habits to snap yourself out of being uncoachable. You can go from being uncoachable to coachable in just a moment. Try it so that you can better explain the process to your clients. Once you become aware of what your triggers are, you can choose a different response and open yourself up to more opportunities for growth.

their time to coach someone who is being uncoachable. Here are a few of their comments:

- ▶ "Generally, I will try two to three sessions to see if they will become receptive over time. However, if they do not feel that they need coaching, I try to end with an open-ended session. 'We really are not making progress—my role is not to push you into something you are not ready for nor want. I am willing to try this again if you change your mind.'" Bonnie S. Turner

- ▶ "Everyone is receptive just maybe not to you. The minute you start blaming the student you should stop coaching. But if you can't succeed (and we all have those situations), you should enthusiastically get the student to a coach who can." Laurence Haughton

- ▶ "It is worth some time to the coach to find what it is about an individual that makes the person uncoachable. In some respects it may be worth some time to the other person to have demonstrated your openness to provide the coaching without an agenda of creating an engagement. A new insight could be the result for both people." John McCabe

- ▶ "It is rarely worth the time. I tend to work only with people who ask for coaching. On those few occasions when I have been involved with someone who is uncoachable (usually performance coaching at the boss's request), I do find that clear, up-front contracting is imperative: here is what you can expect from me, here is what I expect from you, here are the likely consequences if we don't succeed. Can you do that? If not, let's quit right now." Dick Richards

- ▶ "I think it's wrong to conclude that someone is not receptive. Although it may initially look that way, it may be more that you've touched a core issue for them that they need to process privately before coming out the other end. Sometimes this takes a while, but once the seed is planted, ideas continue to sprout even if the coach is no longer part of the conversation." Barry Zweibel

- ▶ "It may be worth other people's time—I cannot speak for them. It is not worth my time. I don't handle these situations at all. I just don't work with people who are not motivated to change. I don't judge these people in any way. It is their lives—not mine. I just don't want to waste my time." Marshall Goldsmith

▶ "No, it is not. However, 95 percent of the people I have met are coachable, and you take the time to find out what motivates them." Tim Ursiny

▶ "Coaching an individual who is not receptive to coaching is a challenge for even the most experienced coaches. Sometimes it is possible to use questioning to reveal the individual's concerns about coaching and to coach around those concerns in order to build rapport and trust. It is possible to work through these concerns and build great coaching relationships; however, coaching an individual who is absolutely unwilling to participate after some attempts can be damaging and needs to be dealt with carefully." Christina Madrid

▶ "It depends. If it is a paying client and our coaching relationship isn't working, I would suggest that we end the relationship. To continue to accept payment for coaching where the person isn't coachable violates a value of mine and takes up time that I could use better. In the workplace, I alter my expectations for coaching depending on the individual." Chris Bailey

▶ "It can be. Usually I've experienced this scenario when people's managers have ordained that they need coaching. My approach has been to ask a lot of questions and to allow the clients to define what they want, not what the boss wants. That way, it transitions from something that is being done 'to them' to something they are doing for themselves—then any resistance falls to the side." Kathleen Ream

As these coaches point out, you want to try to determine why your clients are uncoachable and help them if you can. If your efforts fail, it may be that they would respond more favorably to a different coach or to coaching at another time.

Avoid These Coaching Pitfalls

A goal of coaches should be to help improve client coachability. There are some things that you can do that could get in the way of coachability. Every day, well-meaning coaches get frustrated because their clients are not making progress.

Basic Rule 13
You cannot always improve your client's coachability.

Occasionally, it's the behaviors of the coaches that is turning off or tuning out these clients. Here are a few examples of coaching pitfalls to avoid:

- **Agreeing with your client when another response would be more helpful:** Encouraging a client and providing acknowledgment is important. Coaches should beware of, however, agreeing with clients simply because the clients get defensive or bothered when people don't share their points of view. This is a tricky situation, because you want your clients to be happy and coachable, but you also want them to grow and develop better receptivity. Share which parts of their ideas you feel support their goals and which parts are not in alignment with what they want to achieve.

- **Being judgmental or rigid**: Coaches should avoid being too opinionated when coaching. Feel free to share observations and offer your thoughts and concerns, but resist stating things in black-and-white terms. Coaches need to be flexible and see setbacks as temporary slowdowns in progress. It is not productive nor recommended that you tell clients they are wrong or lazy or that their goals are not worthwhile.

- **Going too fast or slow for your client**: Each client will want to take things at a different pace. Sometimes coaches have a process that does not allow for flexibility. It is more common that the coach wants to takes things slower than the client. You may have exercises or assessments and planning documents you want to use, but be willing and ready to modify your plan for coaching to suit your client's needs.

- **Being untrustworthy**: This point may seem obvious, but many clients never open up to their coaches because they are not comfortable with how the information will be handled. You will want to include a discussion of confidentiality early on, but then you need to be an extraordinary role model of trustworthiness. Be careful what you say about others to your client, too. If you share other conversations you've had, why would your client feel comfortable sharing sensitive information with you?

By falling into these coaching pitfalls, you may be making your job as a coach more difficult and less successful. People are coachable one minute and may be uncoachable the next. Some people will be more fickle than others. By observing the verbal and nonverbal signs of coachability, you should be able to recognize which behaviors work best, and those that might be getting in the way.

The greatest coaching pitfall of all is failing to be a coachable coach. Coaching is a craft, and you will develop your practice over time by listening to and learning from others. The more open you are, the more you will learn. In addition, being a good role model of coachability will help your clients see what coachability looks like and its benefits. The famous quote by Mahatma Gandhi, "You must be the change you seek in the world," sums this sentiment up nicely. Coachability is a way of being; and when you are highly coachable, you have greater access to the ideas and treasures of the world. This is the case for your clients, too. By improving your coachability and employing techniques to help your clients improve coachability, your coaching practice will be set up for greater success.

Getting It Done

For the next three days, take a self-assessment of your feelings and coach-ability three times during the day. Notice how your moods and receptiv-ity ebb and flow throughout the day. Also take note of the triggers that make you less coachable. Use exercise 5-1 as a guide.

In the next chapter, you will learn how to build your clients' self-awareness.

Exercise 5-1. Coachability triggers.

How do you feel right now?

(Circle the statements that match your feelings. Indicate any reasons or triggers.)

I would welcome contrary ideas. Why: Triggers:	I am on the defense. Why: Triggers:
I am interested in new ideas or perspectives. Why: Triggers:	I don't want any new ideas right now. Why: Triggers:
I am in the mood for coaching. Why: Triggers:	I am not in the mood for coaching. Why: Triggers:
I would love to incorporate changes into my plan. Why: Triggers:	I really don't want to change my plan. Why: Triggers:
I would like some additional training, knowledge, or development. Why: Triggers:	I pretty much know what I need to reach this goal. Why: Triggers:
I would like to talk about my weaknesses. Why: Triggers:	I would rather not talk about my weaknesses. Why: Triggers:
I feel like I have had a setback that I can overcome. Why: Triggers:	This failure will be difficult to overcome. Why: Triggers:
I would like to have a discussion about this goal. Why: Triggers:	I would like to think about this goal on my own for a while. Why: Triggers:

6

Building Client Self-Awareness

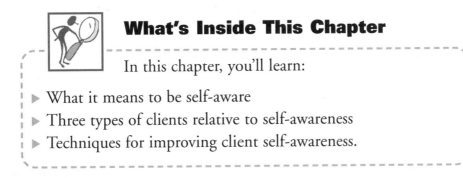

What's Inside This Chapter

In this chapter, you'll learn:

- ▶ What it means to be self-aware
- ▶ Three types of clients relative to self-awareness
- ▶ Techniques for improving client self-awareness.

Coaching Should Enhance Client Self-Awareness

Have you ever worked with a leader like this? Mark is a technically smart leader whom people avoid. Most don't want to talk to Mark nor attend meetings with him. He may know his stuff when it comes to accounting, but he seems to know very little about how relationships work. If you were to coach Mark, one of the greatest gifts you could offer him would be to help him see the effects of his communication style.

A lack of self-awareness is not always linked to unknown weaknesses. Sometimes your clients will not be aware of their strengths. Have you worked with leaders who had amazing talents that they did not recognize? Some might call this humility, but being unaware of strengths can get in the way of hopes, dreams, and goals.

People who have a good sense of their strengths and weaknesses, who are self-aware, are better able to achieve their goals. One of the purposes of coaching is to help clients become more self-aware, so they can focus learning and growth where it will make the greatest difference.

What Does It Mean to Be Self-Aware?

Megan knows that she needs to develop better organization skills and wants to develop better presentation skills. Megan is open to coaching and development. Megan's boss, Chris, sees things a bit differently. Chris thinks that Megan needs to learn to prioritize and delegate more effectively. Chris would also like to see Megan improve her overall business acumen so she could participate more fully in staff meetings. Is Megan self-aware?

Megan is not self-aware. She knows what she thinks are her strengths and weaknesses but does not see her manager's perspective. Your clients may be like Megan. They may come to you and think they know the areas in which they should focus development. They might be wrong. Being self-aware means that you:

▶ Know your strengths and weaknesses.
▶ Understand what's getting in the way of better results and goal attainment.
▶ Hear and understand what your manager believes are your strengths and weaknesses based on how they relate to your goals and responsibilities.
▶ Know how your style and behaviors affect your team members and peers.

In general, being self-aware means knowing the reputation you have built in the organization and the ways in which you can enhance it. Many of your clients

Noted

Clients will have a positive reputation when they are trusted, follow through on promises, produce results, are pleasurable to work with, are knowledgeable, and are viewed as an asset to the company. Clients will suffer from poor reputations if they are not viewed as trustworthy, don't follow through, produce poor or marginal results, are difficult or unpleasant to work with, or are not viewed as credible or talented.

will come to coaching sessions with only a partial view of their reputations and effectiveness. Effective coaching is one of the best tools for improving self-awareness because it is more likely to unearth why clients are successful and ways they can become more effective.

Basic Rule 14

Being self-aware means understanding the reputation you have built and the barriers you face toward meeting your goals. Coaching plays significant roles in helping clients become more self-aware.

What are your clients' frames of reference? The worldliness of their views and experiences will influence your clients' self-awareness. If they have been working for the same company for many years, without exposure to various styles and techniques, their perspectives of what great performance looks like might be narrow. Managers who have worked for poor role models lack adequate reference points and examples from which to self-evaluate their reputations and skills. You can play an important role in broadening your clients' perspectives.

Noted

Your clients' worldliness is a measure of the diversity of their experiences and exposures. Clients who have only worked for one company and one department and who have not participated in professional organizations may have a lower degree of worldliness. Clients who have worked for several companies and have been exposed to many styles and business cultures will be worldlier.

How to Improve Client Self-Awareness

Coaches provide a lifelong service to clients when they help the clients become more self-aware. Information is power, and leaders who are unaware of their potential derailing factors are powerless to improve. To be most helpful, you will need to recognize the signs that indicate clients' levels of self-awareness. Consider these scenarios:

▶ Bob has risen through the ranks and is now in an upper middle management position. Bob's promotions have been a result of his tenure and loyalty to the company. His management and leadership skills are mediocre. His goal is to become a vice president. Bob has a reputation for being emotional and defensive. He does not ask for coaching and becomes uncoachable when offered suggestions in a meeting setting. Bob's managers walk on eggshells around him and do not like working for him. Bob knows that he can get emotional at times, but he does not recognize how poor his reputation is and how this is affecting his goal to become a vice president.

▶ Alexandra means well, but she gets too emotional and defensive, particularly around managers higher in her organization chart. She can be articulate when talking one-on-one with her manager or employees, but is much less effective when challenged by multiple managers or in a group. Alexandra's manager has talked with her about this, and she acknowledges that it happens. She wants to become a more influential, well-regarded manager. Alexandra is frustrated about this and knows that it is harming her reputation. She wants to change but has no idea where to turn.

▶ Lorenzo can drive people crazy. He is impulsive and full of energy. He sees the glass as half empty and has been called "Chicken Little" by co-workers. Even so, Lorenzo is one of the company's best leaders. He pushes himself, his team, and his peers to do their best work by asking many questions and being courageous enough to ask the uncomfortable, but obvious, questions during staff meetings. He knows he can be a bit intense and negative at times and responds well when others point this out to him. Lorenzo wants to become more facilitative and less pushy. He has asked for coaching and training on several occasions and has used what he has learned.

Bob, Alexandra, and Lorenzo have weaknesses that could become derailing factors. Bob has poor self-awareness, but Alexandra and Lorenzo recognize their weaknesses. How should a coach help these and other professionals? These scenarios represent three types of clients: the unaware; the self-aware, but lost; and the self-aware and self-motivated.

Noted

Derailing factors are behavioral habits or skill deficiencies that could endanger success in clients' current positions or the jobs they covet. A derailing factor is often a strength gone to the extreme, like assertiveness that becomes bossiness or cooperativeness that becomes submissiveness. If you can help your clients acknowledge their derailing factors, they will be in much better positions to reach their goals.

Unaware Clients

This is a touchy subject, isn't it? How can a coach help Bob become more self-aware? Bob is also uncoachable much of the time, which makes this a particularly difficult situation. Coaching is likely to be neither welcomed nor effective in Bob's situation for the following reasons:

- ▶ Bob is not being coachable.
- ▶ Bob's goal is not likely the real goal.

Most people who covet titles or positions are really looking for something else. So to help Bob, you should discuss what his interests are. Bob's defensiveness is going to get in the way of him hearing about his derailing factor constructively. Bob needs a proverbial two-by-four effect, which can only come from someone he sees as an authority, like his manager or perhaps a human resources executive.

Noted

Two-by-four effect: When you give someone a two-by-four to the forehead, you are offering direct feedback that is not sugar coated. This approach should be used in only select situations. Some people respond well to direct feedback because it creates dissonance that enlivens the motivation to change. Other people find a two-by-four to the forehead personally devastating.

Self-Aware, but Lost Clients

Alexandra is self-aware, but lost. She knows that her emotional and defensive reactions are getting in the way, and she is motivated to change. However, Alexandra does not know what to do. To enhance self-awareness, you will need to spend several sessions with Alexandra exploring the root causes of her defensive and emotional reactions. Extensive one-on-one coaching that is candid and supportive will benefit self-aware, but lost clients. Group training classes often don't help because the client is likely playing the role of the victim and the conversation that improves this is not likely to occur in a group. Coaching conversations should focus on the goal and the beliefs and behaviors that best support reaching the goal.

Self-Aware and Self-Motivated Clients

Lorenzo is both self-aware and self-motivated. He seeks coaching and development and is eager to try new approaches. To enhance self-awareness, the coach should offer Lorenzo candid coaching to help him meet his development goals. He will likely be interested in any assessments or classes that will further clarify his style and offer insight.

Think About This

Self-aware and self-motivated clients are a pleasure to work with because they are open, eager, and willing to try almost anything. Be careful that you do not let their eagerness get you off track by performing all kinds of self-assessments and arranging for lots of training. You need to ensure that your coaching stays on track and focuses on what will help the clients the most. Self-aware and self-motivated clients will always welcome opportunities to learn more about themselves, but this might not be the best use of their time.

Does this mean that coaches should not try to coach unaware clients? No! Bob's case is extreme, and most situations are not so difficult. To enhance self-awareness for those in the unaware category, ask many open-ended questions and offer self-assessments that nudge the clients into being more aware of their derailing factors. If the clients are receptive to direct feedback, offer an honest and objective assessment of observed behaviors. It is also helpful to clarify the clients' goals and ask them to determine the beliefs that will support achieving their goals.

Think About This

When sharing observations, follow the SAR method—describe the situation, action or behavior, and result observed. Below is an example of how to use this method. Feedback can evoke an emotional response. Your client might get defensive or feel attacked. Because the SAR method focuses your feedback on a specific observation, it is less likely to evoke a negative response.

- **Situation**: You have said that you want to create a more participative environment and encourage your team to share more ideas.
- **Action or behavior**: When you led the staff meeting yesterday, you asked for questions, but your body language said you didn't want feedback. When no one spoke up, you quickly accepted that there was no feedback.
- **Result observed**: Your staff did not participate in the meeting, and you did not get the benefit of hearing their ideas or concerns.

Helping clients improve self-awareness means creating the link between their goals and today's reality. Coaches should talk about derailing factors and other development needs in a way that validates that everyone has them. Clients become more self-aware with open and relaxed conversation. It is important the coaching conversation does

Think About This

Try using self-assessments to help clients gain self-awareness. If only one individual needs the assessment, there are several online or paper resources you can use. If the entire team could benefit from an assessment, then it might be wise to propose a broader effort. Many coaches use the Myers Briggs Type Indicator or a similar behavioral tendencies assessment. These are excellent for defining general tendencies but may not point out specific derailing factors. A thorough 360-degree instrument, like the Profiler from the Center For Creative Leadership, will offer specific information. Most professional 360-degree instruments are lengthy and expensive, but they can be worth the cost if you and your clients use the information and follow up on the feedback received. There is an assessment for every set of skills and topics.

not sound like a performance-management conversation because this will get in the way of progress. Knowing derailing factors is good and opens new possibilities.

There are many ways that you can help your clients build self-awareness. You will want to focus on techniques that improve your clients' knowledge of their reputations and ways that improve their overall worldliness. Table 6-1 lists several techniques that can help improve your clients' self-awareness.

As a coach, you have the opportunity to take a bird's-eye view of your clients' strengths, weaknesses, and barriers to success. If you can help your clients eliminate

Table 6-1. Techniques for improving client self-awareness.

Purpose	Techniques
To improve your clients' knowledge and understanding of their reputations within organizations	Help your clients prepare for and follow through with open and detailed conversations with their managers.
	Help your clients analyze setbacks and disappointments.
	Help your clients design feedback sessions to collect perspectives from team members and peers.
	Use assessments that are appropriate for your clients' needs and goals.
	Provide open and detailed feedback about what you have observed.
To improve your clients' business worldliness	Expose your clients to fresh thinking through articles, organization meetings, blog posts, books, and television programs.
	Help your clients create and implement plans for broadening the type of projects in which they participate.
	Help your clients build their professional networks with people outside of the company.
	Help your clients find and connect with internal mentors who can offer new or diverse perspectives.

just one derailing factor and broaden their perspectives, it could make a big differ-ence. It is very satisfying to see clients' proverbial lightbulbs shine bright—when they see something in a new way and a world of possibilities.

Getting It Done

Assess your reputation using exercise 6-1. Interview two or three trusted colleagues or your manager. Reflect on what you learn about yourself, and think about how you might use this tool with clients.

Exercise 6-1. Learn about your reputation.

Reputation Survey

For each trait listed, indicate my ability level. If a weakness, do not hesitate to point this out. Also rank these traits, 1 being the trait I am strongest in and 7 being the trait I am weakest in.

Quality, Trait, or Habit	Strength	Average	Weakness	Rank
Timelines of work and projects				
Reliability				
Easy to work with, even when times are difficult				
Acts quickly and follows up				
Results orientation				
Technical skills				
Builds and maintains relationships				

Share a time when I let you down at work.

Share the most important contribution I have made to the business in the last year.

(continued on page 76)

Exercise 6-1. Learn about your reputation (continued).

What has been my greatest failure in the last year?
How well do you believe I represent you and your interests?
How productive do I appear to be? Highly productive, satisfactorily productive, or below average in productivity?
What do you like most and least about working with me? Most: Least:

In the next chapter, you will explore ways to help your clients get unstuck.

7

Helping Clients
Get Unstuck

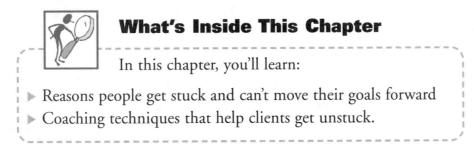

What's Inside This Chapter

In this chapter, you'll learn:

▶ Reasons people get stuck and can't move their goals forward
▶ Coaching techniques that help clients get unstuck.

Why People Get Stuck

When you are stuck, you feel drained and frustrated. Your brain finds it difficult to get engaged and your fingers struggle to type the right words. You can be stuck in one area and seemingly effective in another. For example, many professionals can zoom forward with many projects at a time while avoiding and getting nowhere on another project. You might be successful at work, but failing to move forward on your goal to own a company. Sometimes being stuck affects all areas of your work or life because of the connection to your self-esteem. Everyone gets stuck.

The root of the stuckness is often mental and easy to dislodge with the right catalyst. Coaching is a great way to help clients who are bogged down or unable to move goals or projects forward. Clients may be stuck because they are

- overwhelmed and can't move forward
- drowning in victim conversations
- feeling disconnected from goals
- mentally drained and exhausted
- suffering from a vague or ill-defined vision
- not in action
- trying to do everything
- committed to the wrong path
- uncoachable.

A proactive coach can help clients get things rolling again. Helping a client get unstuck is a valuable gift that makes a big difference to the successes and productivity of your clients and the organizations. This type of coaching serves clients' immediate needs and builds their capabilities to prevent getting stuck in the future.

Think About This

Create a list of tasks or projects that you want to accomplish, but are having a hard time moving forward. Look at the list of reasons people get stuck and try to determine which symptom applies to each task or project. Notice any trends?

Coaching should help clients get unstuck. To do this you will need to recognize when your clients are stuck and diagnose the best remedy. Here is the list of situations that can cause clients to get stuck, this time with suggestions for how to help your clients overcome the causes of being stuck.

Overwhelmed and Can't Move Forward

Clients who feel overwhelmed often lack organization, plans, or processes. It may also be that they have procrastinated or overcommitted themselves and need to bring in extra help. The feeling of being overwhelmed can also be a result of doing work that is not engaging. When you have 10 interesting projects to complete, you feel challenged and excited. When you have 10 uninspiring projects, you feel overwhelmed and stuck.

Your clients need to get organized and in action. If there are projects they don't want to do, they should try to renegotiate or find a way they can get excited about the work and get on with it. It might be wise for them to get temporary help. You can also help your clients ensure that they are working on the right tasks. Many overwhelmed people suffer from an inability to delegate and prioritize. They accept too many meeting requests and handle every issue instead of delegating or planning. Your clients might benefit from time-management classes or from renegotiating their roles and priorities with their managers.

Drowning in Victim Conversations

A victim conversation gets in the way of progress by giving your clients reasons to remain stuck. Here are a few examples of victim statements:

- It's not my fault.
- I have been trying my hardest.
- How could I have predicted this?
- It's out of my hands.
- This is not my lucky day.

Victim conversations may or may not be true. Your clients may have suffered from setbacks or what seems like bad luck. They may have experienced losses. You will want to empathize with your clients, but you still want to help them to stop playing victims. When it comes to goal attainment, whether the victim conversations are true does not matter. They are unhelpful and do not serve your clients' goals. Although it might be true that the clients could not have predicted a change that caused a setback, dwelling on this is unhelpful. If your clients are stuck in victim conversations, acknowledge the situation, but then transition the conversations toward exploring the beliefs that they could adopt that would be helpful in getting things rolling again. One caveat: These suggestions apply to general business situations and not serious mental problems that are better dealt with by a professional therapist.

Basic Rule 15

Victim conversations, although sometimes true, are not helpful and get in the way of goal attainment. Coaches help their clients change their dialogues to be more actionable and empowering.

Think About This

Victim conversations are a common barrier to success and cause of stuckness. They may even be common in the organization culture (based on assumptions of powerlessness and being affected by the past). Start noticing your own self-talk, and catch yourself thinking about frustrations or goals from a victim's perspective. Reframe your conversations and thinking, and notice what this does for your outlook and your energy level. Victim conversations are draining.

Feeling Disconnected From Goals

Clients may get stuck when their goals are poorly defined or something has changed that affects the goals. If their day-to-day actions do not support their goals, they eventually lose focus. Help your clients redefine their goals to make them inspiring and meaningful, and then help align their activities to better support achieving the goals. This will also ensure they communicate their goals with others.

How do you know if your clients are disconnected from their goals? One indication is their ability to articulate their goals succinctly. If they speak in past and future tenses, but not in present tense, then they might not be present to the goals. Another indication of a disconnected goal is a lack of passion or drive toward achieving it. Help the clients recall why the goals were important, and reinvent and update the goals to something they can get excited about.

Mentally Drained and Exhausted

People have a finite amount of mental energy. There is a difference between making time and taking time to work on goals. Making time means adding on to your to-do list and often leads to mental exhaustion. Taking time means setting aside time to work on projects that matter and removing other tasks from your to-do list. Help your clients make choices about time that ensure they work on the most important tasks and eliminate tasks from their to-do lists that are not great uses of their time. Provide coaching that helps them say *no* more often.

Even your most organized clients need to take mental breaks now and then. If your clients are stuck because they have been charging ahead for too long and are worn out, help them see they need to take well-deserved breaks. It might also be beneficial for them to modify their schedule to include more time to reflect and recharge. Help your clients understand that they cannot do their best thinking when they are exhausted.

Noted

There is a difference between making time and taking time. When you make time, you add on to your day and to-do list. When you take time, you set time aside within your day and take other tasks off the list.

Suffering From a Vague or Ill-Defined Vision

A vague vision of the future is hard to act on. Examples of vague visions are "provide for my family" or "help the company improve profitability." Help your clients crisp up their visions by asking open-ended questions that enable the clients to create actionable visions. Many leaders will express a goal of "becoming a better leader." This is a noble notion, but is neither helpful nor inspiring. Goals should be meaningful and exciting. Each leader will have strengths and weaknesses. Help tie leadership skills in with business opportunities or problems. Perhaps team communication and development is a challenge and will become critical as significant changes are implemented. Here are a couple of leadership development goals that are more specific and actionable:

- ▶ Over the next six months, I want to provide the coaching and support that will enable my team to prepare for the coming changes such that we have the skills and are eager and willing to support the new products.
- ▶ During the next year, I want to work with my team to realign the department's processes, procedures, projects, and practices to best support the overall corporate strategies.

Not in Action

A lack of action is a common reason for being stuck and is often combined with other barriers. Why are your clients not in action? Determine what is getting in the way. Help your clients brainstorm lists of potential actions, and then select those actions that will make the greatest differences. To create robust lists, ask your clients to play devil's advocates and see the situations from different viewpoints. It might be beneficial to facilitate group brainstormings. Ask for agreements about when the clients will take each action, and follow up. Challenge your clients to take actions in support of their goals every day. If the added structure is helpful and welcomed, have them email you their daily actions. Actions can start very small. Once the momentum starts, each action will reinforce the next and lead to larger actions.

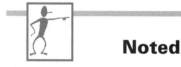

Noted

Playing devil's advocate means sharing ideas from the opposing side of the argument.

Trying to Do Everything

Clients may get stuck because they have failed to enroll others in their goals or ask for support. Amazing things can happen when clients share their visions for the future. Help your clients get their goals into the world and get the processes started by which they receive input and feedback from others. Suggest that clients share their goals with two people per day for one week. They will be amazed at the results of sharing their goals. People want to help others and will often offer support and enroll in the goals' successful implementations. Clients who are introverts might resist taking this coaching more than extroverts. Offer suggestions for ways they can share their goals that are less confrontational, like sending emails.

Committed to the Wrong Path

Some clients get stuck because they are on the wrong track. Have they taken actions without results? Are they inadvertently going backward? Many well-meaning and dedicated people waste time on goals and approaches that lead in the opposite direction of their desires, needs, and intentions. Sometimes this is because of naivete, or lack of knowledge, and sometimes this occurs because the path was once right. Help your clients connect their goals, actions, and results together. By tracking their results, clients will be able to see when implementations are working.

Uncoachable

Being uncoachable can lead to being stuck because you are not getting the input and ideas you need. In addition to the specific suggestions in chapter 5, here are several ideas to get clients unstuck:

▶ Change their conversations. Conversations create reality. To improve their realities, clients may need to change what they are talking about. To create change, they will want to increase the number and quality of conversations about the change.

▶ Tap in to new ideas and talents. It is often helpful to generate additional ideas and perspectives that can re-energize their commitments and enhance their lists of potential actions.

▶ Put a stake in the ground. Goals can seem unattainable and far away unless there are milestones.

▶ Make requests that improve the project's momentum.

Basic Rule 16
Getting stuck is common. Coaches should help clients identify their barriers and suggest ways the clients can get unstuck.

Getting stuck is a temporary event and can be relatively harmless with the right coaching to get clients going again. If you help your clients distinguish and reduce stuckness, you will help them succeed today and tomorrow. In time, your clients will learn to recognize when they are stuck and help themselves get moving again. To get unstuck, it is important to try something new—get in action in a different way.

Coaching Techniques That Help Clients Get Unstuck

Here is a summary of the coaching techniques mentioned throughout this chapter. You will want to select the actions that will most help your clients get unstuck. Each client will be at a different place in development and will benefit from an individualized approach to coaching. This is part of the art of coaching. Here are the techniques:

- Help your clients get organized and in action. Coach them on how to re-negotiate tasks they do not have time to complete.
- Review your clients' to-do lists, and help them ensure they are working on the right tasks. Suggest techniques or trainings that will help them delegate and prioritize.
- Help your clients replace victim conversations with productive conversations about what they can do to get the project back on track. You can do this by asking provocative and evocative questions that allow your clients to explore options they had not previously considered.
- Help your clients define their goals in clear terms. Ask them questions to determine whether the goals they select are inspiring and motivating for them.
- Encourage clients to take a mental break when needed. Help them plan for the break so that they will feel comfortable and relaxed.
- Suggest leadership trainings that will tie in to your clients' business opportunities or problems.
- Help your clients brainstorm lists of potential actions, and then select those actions that will make the greatest differences.
- Offer to facilitate team brainstorming meetings.
- Ask for an agreement about which actions your clients will take. Follow up on these agreements, and discuss any barriers.
- Challenge your clients to take actions in support of their goals every day. If the added structure is helpful and welcomed, have them email you their daily actions.
- Help your clients communicate their goals by discussing ways and reasons to share goals. Suggest they share their goals with two people every day for one week.
- Discuss your clients' goals to ensure they are connected to their actions and the results they have been asked to achieve. Ask provocative and evocative questions to determine the level of alignment between goals and actions. Suggest ways they can track their progress.
- Shift the coaching conversations to enable coachability. Recognize and avoid the situations that trigger uncoachability.

▶ Help your clients brainstorm requests and actions that will enable progress.

▶ Brainstorm milestones and smaller, short-term goals that support your clients' overall goals.

Everyone gets stuck. When people stay stuck, goals go nowhere. Others free themselves and get moving again. A great coach can help accelerate the process of getting things back on track.

Getting It Done

Use exercise 7-1 to diagnose what is causing your clients to be stuck and to identify potential remedies.

Exercise 7-1. Diagnostic suggestions for helping your client get unstuck.

Is Your Client...	Potential Remedies	Your Action Plan
Overwhelmed and can't move forward	• Help your client get organized. Help your client get in action. Determine if temporary help is needed.	
Drowning in victim conversations	• Help your client acknowledge and transition out of victim conversations. Help your client select and take on better beliefs.	
Feeling disconnected from goals	• Help your client redefine goals to make them inspiring and meaningful, and then help align activities to better support achieving the goals. Ensure the client communicates goals with others.	
Mentally drained and exhausted	• Help your client make better choices about how to spend time. Provide coaching that helps your client say *no* more often.	
Suffering from a vague or ill-defined vision	• Ask open-ended questions that enable your client to crisp up and create an actionable vision.	

(continued on page 86)

Exercise 7-1. Diagnostic suggestions for helping your client get unstuck (continued).

Is Your Client...	Potential Remedies	Your Action Plan
Not in action	• Determine what is getting in the way of action. Help your client brainstorm a list of potential actions, and select those that will make the greatest difference. Help your client make requests that will improve the project's momentum.	
Trying to do everything	• Help your clients share their goals and receive input and feedback from others. Suggest they share their goals with two people per day for one week. Help your clients determine ways to share goals that feel comfortable for them.	
Committed to the wrong path	• Measure results of actions, and test goals for relevancy and effectiveness. Challenge the status quo if it does not seem to be working any longer.	
Uncoachable	• Determine what's triggering the uncoachability. Help your client recognize uncoachability and offer techniques for being more coachable. Help your client redefine success.	

In the next chapter, you will learn techniques that can help your clients generate breakthroughs in results.

8

Facilitating Breakthroughs

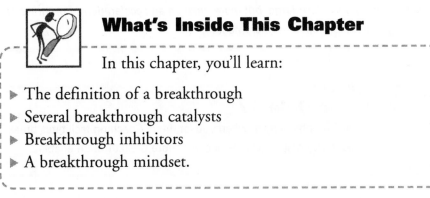

What's Inside This Chapter

In this chapter, you'll learn:

▶ The definition of a breakthrough
▶ Several breakthrough catalysts
▶ Breakthrough inhibitors
▶ A breakthrough mindset.

Coaching is at its best when it facilitates a breakthrough. Breakthroughs happen when clients let them. Sometimes clients are like sponges, happily soaking in new information. All too often, however, preconceived notions, fears, and egos shut out the opportunities that they seek. This is normal, and you can help your clients recognize ways to get beyond the barriers to breakthroughs.

Seeing the aha moment occur, the lightbulb go on, or the brain synapses fire like crazy is a wonderful experience for a coach. There is no better feeling than knowing you supported your clients in ways that enabled breakthroughs. You can feel the joy, energy, and focus from these moments. After breakthroughs occur, reality shifts and your clients feel closer to achieving their goals.

Noted

The term breakthrough *means different things to different people. Some reserve the word for describing scientific discoveries and efforts worthy of the Nobel Prize. Others believe they have breakthroughs many times a week. A broad definition of breakthroughs helps generate them. If you thought a breakthrough was something rare, elusive, and unlikely, you would not experience as many. A breakthrough is*

- *a moment when someone receives an insight, aha, idea, cognitive snap (relative to the preceding period), or epiphany*
- *progress experienced by an individual or small group*
- *a discontinuous, positive change or a leap forward in thinking, action, or results*
- *a change that can be small or large, but there must be an acceleration of progress or sudden insight (transformative vs. incremental).*

Basic Rule 17

Breakthroughs happen when you let them. Coaching facilitates breakthroughs by helping clients become more breakthrough enabled.

The road toward a breakthrough can be short and straight or long and winding. To help clients produce breakthroughs that help them achieve or beat their goals, you should understand the breakthrough catalysts, inhibitors, and mindset. Armed with this knowledge, you can ask better questions and suggest paths that help clients increase activities in support of their goals.

Breakthrough Catalysts

Breakthroughs occur in various circumstances. Breakthrough catalysts are conditions that often precede and facilitate breakthroughs. There are many potential breakthrough catalysts, and they will vary by individual. Share this list with your clients, and ask them to define their common breakthrough catalysts.

Dissonance Experiences

Some breakthroughs happen when people experience cognitive dissonance. Failed attempts, rejections, and embarrassments may cause clients to question what they are doing and explore new possibilities. Although they do not hope for failures to occur, the clients can use these experiences to progress and enjoy breakthroughs. If clients take on a defensive or uncoachable stance, a breakthrough is unlikely.

Noted

Dissonance is a condition of conflict or anxiety resulting from inconsistency between clients' beliefs and their actions or results—for example, an unexpected failure.

Taking Action

Getting in action is a great way to create momentum and put goals and intentions into the world—an important step in creating breakthroughs. Many of the breakthrough catalysts are also forms of taking action. Taking action means trying something new, being proactive, or doing what has been put off. Progress suffers when people are reactive.

Deep Thinking

Some people use mental retreats to generate new ideas, refocus, and tap in to their goals. Deep thinking includes mountaintop thinking, playing around with ideas, talking to yourself, and noticing things in new ways.

Coached Nudges

Breakthroughs facilitated by coached nudges are very common. In fact, most breakthroughs occur following worthwhile conversations. When coaches, peers, friends, managers, or strangers say just what people need to hear, the conversations are special gifts. When the clients are open to them, coached nudges can facilitate breakthroughs.

Making Requests

Making requests is perhaps the easiest and fastest way to produce breakthroughs. Mahatma Gandhi said, "If you don't ask, you don't get." It is important to make requests that will make a difference and enable progress. There are two types of requests to consider:

- Everyday requests—reasonable, modest, helpful
- Prime requests—a tad beyond what is reasonable, would make a significant difference if granted.

Both everyday and prime requests are helpful and should be a regular part of your clients' daily and weekly practices. The more prime requests clients make, the better their chances for exciting breakthroughs. Prime requests will be turned down more often, but the few that are granted will make disproportionately higher, positive effects.

Think About This

To see the power of requests, make five requests every week related to your goals—the bigger the request the better. Making requests does not mean you are selfish nor greedy. The requests help move your goals forward and increase your contribution to the organization. Once you have tried this for a few weeks and enjoyed the benefits (maybe breakthroughs), you will be in a better position to coach your clients about how to make requests.

Changing or Realigning the Context

One of the most effective ways to bring about a breakthrough is for your clients to adjust their contexts. In his book, *The Tipping Point*, Malcolm Gladwell (2002) wrote about how the New York City crime rate plummeted in the 1990s, enabled in large part by changes made to the context. Implementing the Broken Windows theory, the city cleaned the graffiti off subway cars and stopped subway riders from jumping the turnstiles. By changing the look and feel of the subway experience, the crime rate decreased.

A change in context can have a dramatic influence on perspective. Changing the context might mean creating a workspace that is pleasant and relaxed. The ancient practice of feng shui seeks to align surrounding elements to the goals of each space. Even those who do not follow feng shui will likely acknowledge that a cluttered workspace often accompanies a cluttered mind. Another example of a context change is exploring unknown surroundings to broaden thinking and perspectives. Asking a new group of people to brainstorm solutions to a problem is a contextual change.

Think About This

Changing the context is an easy and effective way to make new things happen. Is your workspace cluttered? Are you lunching with intelligent people who make you think? When was the last time you asked an industry leader whom you admire for his or her perspective? Is your workspace energizing or depressing? Consider ways to improve your context, and keep context in mind when you are coaching your clients.

Incubation or Time Away

Many people say that their best thinking occurs when they take a mental break from working on a problem or goal. There is such a thing as overthinking something, and taking a break can help clients forget or set aside assumptions and mental sets that might be getting in the way of progress. Perhaps their brains need a rest, and perhaps they are not resting at all. Some people believe the unconscious mind continues to work on a solution while the conscious mind focuses elsewhere. In either case, it is sometimes more fruitful to take a breather.

Breakthrough catalysts provide a spark that can enable increased progress and breakthroughs. Which catalysts work best for you? To develop your ability to use breakthrough catalysts while coaching, try using them yourself. Experiment with different methods and tools, and notice how each affects your ability to move your goals forward. Here are a few ways you can use the breakthrough catalysts:

▶ Set a goal to take two actions that support your goal every day. These actions can be tiny or significant.

▶ Get away for a day or half-day to a place that is peaceful and stimulating. Reflect and relax. Take a journal or notebook to capture your thoughts and ideas.

▶ Get into conversations about your goal. Talk to two people each day about your goal, inviting them to share ideas and input.

▶ Make two requests that support your goal every day for one week. Ask people you do not know, but should, for a coffee or telephone conversation. Ask your manager or peers to support a change that would help you reach your goal. Ask experts to share their ideas. Ask to be included on a project team. Ask for a change in jobs.

▶ Change your context by joining a new organization or asking a different group of people to a brainstorming meeting. Visit the competition. Read a book by a radical thinker. Read a magazine you would have never thought of buying.

▶ Take time away from the goal or problem. Enjoy your free time. Take a vacation. Take a break in the middle of the afternoon to take a walk and get a fancy coffee drink. Soak in the coffeehouse atmosphere.

Recognizing and using breakthrough catalysts can add velocity to your clients' journeys toward meeting their goals. Notice the catalysts that work for your clients, and share ideas for ways they can put the catalysts to work for them.

Breakthrough Inhibitors

Breakthrough catalysts improve conditions for a breakthrough. Breakthrough inhibitors get in the way and make breakthroughs less likely. To take advantage of and have the mental energy to use breakthrough catalysts, help your clients identify and reduce the number of breakthrough inhibitors getting in the way.

Measure 100 Times, Never Cut

You've heard the saying, "measure twice, cut once," right? That's good advice, but some people take this idea too far. Often called paralysis by analysis, this breakthrough inhibitor gets in the way because, while analysis is action, too much analysis does not lead to forward movement. This is particularly the case for analysis that does not move outside the context (a breakthrough catalyst).

A Focus on Logic

Breakthroughs, by definition, might be a surprise or something unexpected. Therefore, if your clients only do what is logical and familiar, they will reduce the number of possible breakthroughs. Progress follows a path paved by logical and not so logical developments. When collecting and considering ideas and approaches, your clients should not worry about whether something is logical. There will be time to question the viability of the idea, after they've played with the concepts a bit.

A Scarcity Mindset

Some people are less in tune with what's possible. They try one idea and then get discouraged if it does not work. They think it is wrong to make requests to move goals forward. They live in mental paradigms that are focused on limits and reasons not to branch out and be creative. Their socially constructed realities include scarce resources and few possibilities. Clients with this perspective drastically reduce their opportunities for breakthroughs.

Fear

Fear affects everyone at some point. When clients let fear get in the way, they eliminate many possibilities. They should not become reckless, but most fears have nothing to do with impending danger and are likely rooted in a need to be right or save face. In his classic book, *How to Win Friends and Influence People*, Dale Carnegie (1936) suggests that 99 percent of worries don't come true.

The Self-Fulfilling Prophecy

The self-fulfilling prophecy can be helpful or unhelpful. When clients assume that they will fail and never experience breakthroughs, they are often right. The clients' failures occur not because those were the likely outcomes, but because their brains were tuned for defeat. To combat the negative self-fulfilling prophecy, clients need to pay attention to and reprogram destructive self-talk. By acknowledging the power of the self-fulfilling prophecy, clients can create and employ a more positive model.

No Room at the Mental Inn

Attention is a limited resource. There is a limited amount of information anyone can process at any given time. Most people know this, and yet they don't carve out time

Noted

Self-fulfilling prophecy or Pygmalion Effect: Once you establish an expectation, even if it isn't accurate, you act in ways that are consistent with that expectation. Your expectations often determine what becomes reality.

to think and create new ideas. There is a difference between making time and taking time. When you make time, you are adding on to the workday and may go beyond your mental energy capacity. When you take time, you are setting time aside in the day, not adding to the workday. When you have no room at the mental inn, you are not available to receive the information that could result in a breakthrough.

Schools of Thought

People have beliefs and assumptions about how things ought to go. When their schools of thought are limiting and narrowing the range of possibilities, the thoughts get in the way of breakthroughs. To combat this breakthrough inhibitor, clients need to expand their influences and conversations. Suggest that your clients invite a diversity of people to the dialogue, try a new approach, or attend a class taught and attended by people they do not know.

You will notice that many of these breakthrough inhibitors can also be good habits in some situations. For example, being logical is often desirable, but a preoccupation with all things logical can get in the way. As you are coaching, you need to recognize when a good thing has become a barrier and help your clients see this as well. Here are several suggestions for minimizing various breakthrough inhibitors:

▸ Help clients establish if/then contingencies that enable them to move on when all the data is not known. Create a list of actions that can be taken concurrently with analysis and data gathering to improve forward momentum.

▸ Establish a process for collecting ideas and input without judgment or scrutiny. Help your clients experience different contexts before their preconceived notions take over.

▸ Share examples that illustrate a wide range of possibilities. Offer your clients articles and books or suggest Webinars that will open up their perspectives about what's possible. Ask questions that identify potential paths and positive outcomes.

▸ Help your clients realistically identify worst-case scenarios when they seem stuck by unrealistic fears. Help your clients take small steps at first to build confidence for larger actions.

▸ Ask questions that uncover destructive self-talk. Help clients identify messages that better serve their goals. Be sure to notice and share observations about negative self-talk.

▸ Help your clients create a schedule that allows for adequate focus and concentration. Help them evaluate how they spend time and reduce low-value tasks. Suggest books or training programs that develop time management and planning skills.

▸ Expose your clients to new or different mindsets or schools of thought. Recommend movies, books, blogs, magazines, or training programs that you think will widen and enrich their thinking.

Breakthrough inhibitors affect everyone. Help your clients recognize what's getting in the way, and offer suggestions to reduce their barriers. Combining knowledge and intentional actions will go a long way to helping your clients become breakthrough enabled.

Breakthrough Mindset and Habits

To produce breakthroughs, you need to align your thinking and actions such that they optimally support your goals. The breakthrough mindset is a set of beliefs that enables more breakthroughs by using breakthrough catalysts and minimizing breakthrough inhibitors. It's a mindset that will serve most clients very well, but you will want to tweak and customize these beliefs as appropriate. By taking on these beliefs, your clients' heads and hearts will be primed for amazing things to happen.

Basic Rule 18
Breakthroughs are more likely to occur when breakthrough catalysts are employed and breakthrough inhibitors are reduced.

Breakthrough habits are the actions that naturally follow when you take a more powerful mindset. Each belief can lead to many actions, so the possible number of breakthrough habits is unlimited. Your clients can choose aligned actions that suit their styles and preferences. What's most important is that your clients adopt powerful mindsets and that they take actions aligned with the mindset. Beyond this, the specifics can be flexible. People who are in action and engaged will experience more breakthroughs than those who sit back and wait for something to happen. Table 8-1 offers several beliefs that make up the breakthrough mindset and examples of aligned breakthrough habits.

Table 8-1. Beliefs and actions that facilitate breakthroughs.

Breakthrough Mindset	Breakthrough Habits
It is not helpful when I play the victim.	Snap out of funks, poor moods, or bouts of frustration—quickly. Get and stay in action.
Failure and dissonance can lead to progress when I learn from the experience.	Ask for and appreciate opposing views and contrary thoughts.
If my goals are not progressing, I need to get in action (the right actions).	Collect many ideas from various sources. Try new things.
The more I talk about my goals and intentions, the more likely it will be that people will make important connections that help my goals move forward.	Master the art of great dialogue. Broadly share your goals and intentions.
If I am stalled, I might need to change my context or adopt a new paradigm.	Change your context as needed. (If you are stalled, it's needed.) Feed your curiosities!
I need to manage my mental energy.	Take time (not make time) to reflect, relax, and create new ideas.
The more coachable I am, the better the coaching I will receive. The right coaching can make a huge difference.	Ask for and appreciate coaching.
I won't get what I don't ask for.	Make at least five requests related to your goals each week.
My goals are worthy and meaningful and deserve my attention and commitment.	Seek breakthroughs without feeling entitled to them. Make your goals a priority.

If your clients want to change their results, they need to adjust their beliefs so the beliefs are in greater support of their goals. These beliefs support actions aligned with making new things happen. When they practice breakthrough habits, clients will experience more breakthroughs and enjoy greater success. These habits are also beneficial for getting unstuck and improving coachability. Give them a try!

Facilitating a breakthrough feels great. Review and think about breakthrough catalysts, breakthrough inhibitors, and the breakthrough mindset and habits before and after you coach clients. Incorporate techniques that facilitate breakthroughs into the suggestions and action plans you create with your clients. Share resources that are provocative and stimulating. Ask questions that expand your clients' perspectives. Coaches who help their clients recognize breakthrough catalysts and inhibitors, take on breakthrough mindsets, and practice breakthrough habits will enable the clients to experience surprising successes.

Getting It Done

One of the best ways to learn and understand the techniques that will enable breakthroughs is to try them. Some techniques are deceptively simple yet offer huge rewards.

Try this daily practice for one week: Each day, share your goal with two people, take two actions in support of your goal, and make two requests. Exercise 8-1 is a worksheet you can use to chart your actions and progress.

Exercise 8-1. The daily practice for facilitating breakthroughs.

My goal:_____

Day of the Week	Element	What I Did
Monday	Share goal with two people. Make two requests. Take two actions.	
Tuesday	Share goal with two people. Make two requests. Take two actions.	

(continued on page 98)

Exercise 8-1. The daily practice for facilitating breakthroughs (continued).

Day of the Week	Element	What I Did
Wednesday	Share goal with two people.	
	Make two requests.	
	Take two actions.	
Thursday	Share goal with two people.	
	Make two requests.	
	Take two actions.	
Friday	Share goal with two people.	
	Make two requests.	
	Take two actions.	

In the next chapter, you will explore several coaching topics that are beyond the basics.

9

Beyond the Basics

What's Inside This Chapter

In this chapter, you'll learn:

▶ About team coaching
▶ Ways to use technology for coaching
▶ About coaching certification and training programs
▶ Special considerations for executive coaching.

Team Coaching

Coaching a small team of people has many benefits. First, the members of the team become more aware and supportive of each other's goals. This sets up a collaborative and open environment within the team. Another benefit is that people are more likely to do the work and take action between coaching sessions if they know they will be sharing their successes with the group. Team coaching generates healthy peer pressure and heightens each individual's sense of responsibility. Team coaching is an efficient way to provide coaching. You can influence up to 10 people at once. It is also a fun and energizing way to coach.

Basic Rule 19

Coaching a small team of people is a great way to increase your reach as a coach and create a supportive and reinforcing environment.

Team coaching also comes with limitations. If you have a client who would benefit from the proverbial two-by-four effect, as Bob did in chapter 6, this is difficult to do in a group setting unless the members of the group agreed to and are open to such direct public feedback. Team coaching works best when the group has already established trusting and healthy relationships. Though it is possible to start with a team of people who do not know each other, you will need to spend several sessions helping them build relationships. If the team knows each other but lacks mutual respect and trust, you should not try to coach them as a team because they will not be open nor comfortable with each other.

The focus of team coaching is often work-related goals. Each person can have different goals or the team can be working toward a common goal. If you are asked to provide team coaching using a common goal, make sure the team shares this goal. It might be the case that the manager wants people to take on the goal, but some of the team members don't care about the goal. You need to tap in to a goal that each person genuinely wants to achieve.

Here is an example of a real, team-coaching situation: Tim, a department head, asked Lydia to provide team coaching for his five managers. Lydia asked Tim if he wanted the coaching to focus on individual goals or a shared team goal. Tim suggested that the coaching sessions focus on individual goals. This team of managers had productive working relationships. Lydia gathered the group together and helped each person define and articulate a goal to focus on throughout the coaching process. The overall goal was to enable the managers to produce a breakthrough relative to their goals. The coaching sessions were planned for two hours per week for six weeks. Of the six participants (Tim and his five managers), four made excellent progress and two experienced breakthroughs.

The preferred number of people for team-coaching sessions is under 10, and five or six is ideal. This size allows for good dialogue and input and is small enough to permit personalized attention. The coach will need to be able to facilitate group participation and contribution before offering team coaching. Other facilitation tools, like establishing ground rules and agendas, are helpful as well. Team coaching is not a good tool for turning around a dysfunctional team because most dysfunctional teams suffer from poor relationships and a lack of mutual respect. When you first try team coaching, target small teams that have already established and built positive relationships.

Technology for Coaches

To reach your clients and meet their communication needs, you will want to employ a variety of methods. Luckily, there are many technology-based tools that can enhance your coaching practice. As businesses become more global and geographically dispersed, in-person coaching may not be practical nor possible. Although meeting in person is optimal, there are many other ways you can connect with your clients:

- ▶ Phone: Coaching sessions can be conducted over the phone and are particularly suited to sessions where visuals are not needed.
- ▶ Voice Over Internet Protocol (VoIP): Many companies are now using VoIP as a regular communication tool. With VoIP, you can contact your clients anywhere you have an Internet connection. Another advantage of VoIP is that many programs allow file transfer, which allows you to send documents back and forth as you are talking without having to send a separate email.
- ▶ Online Meeting Programs: As travel becomes more expensive and less desirable, many companies are using online meeting platforms to have virtual meetings. If your company subscribes to an online meeting vendor (Microsoft Live Meeting or WebEx, for example), then using this tool for coaching is a great option. During your virtual meeting, you can share documents and actively collaborate. This is also a good tool for small, team-coaching sessions.
- ▶ Email: Although you should not rely on email for all your coaching meetings, it is a good tool to use to keep in touch with your clients between meetings. You should send follow-up emails after each coaching session to clarify and reinforce agreements made during the session. You should also forward interesting articles or blog posts to your clients as you find them.
- ▶ Goal Setting and Project Management Software: If your clients are already familiar with using project management tools, incorporate them into your coaching. There are many project management and goal-setting programs to choose from depending on the size and complexity of the projects or goals.

Examples of programs include GoalPro, GoalMaker, Life Pan Writer, Single-step, ManagePro, FranklinCovey PlanPlus, AceProject, and Microsoft Project.

Think About This

Most software companies offer free trial versions, so test several before you buy. Make sure the program you select will be easy for you and your clients to use. Many Web-based programs are ideal for collaboration and can be accessed anywhere there's an Internet connection.

By using various tools and methods for coaching, you will improve communication effectiveness and serve your clients better. New technology is created for coaches each year, so stay abreast of the latest tools by subscribing to coaching newsletters and reading periodicals that cover coaching. (Many training, organization development, and human resources periodicals cover coaching topics.)

Coaching Certification and Training Programs

As you develop your coaching practice, consider whether a coaching certification program is right for you. There are several national programs and many universities that offer coaching certificates. Each program will vary in length and depth. You will want to weigh your needs, available time, and resources before selecting a program.

The International Coach Federation offers three levels of credential: the Associate Certified Coach, the Professional Certified Coach, and the Master Certified Coach. Each level of certification requires a certain number of coaching and training hours. These programs are for professional coaches.

Coach U's coaching training programs range in length and depth and are well known in the field of coaching. Many of its programs are designed to prepare students to become certified coaches.

Other companies, such as Coach Training University and 1 to 1 Coach Training, offer certification training programs. Many of these programs are costly, so you will want to make sure the program you choose is serving your career goals as a coach.

Think About This

Many universities and training organizations will allow you to take individual courses before committing to a more comprehensive program. This is a good option because you will want to make sure the training is a good fit for you. Try several types of training, including traditional courses, online learning, self-paced courses, and one-on-one coaching.

You may also find degree programs and individual classes at your local university. For example, the Leadership Institute of Seattle offers a master's degree program in coaching. There are also online training programs to choose from, like those at the Career Coach Institute. General training organizations, like American Management Association, and coaching professionals, like Marshall Goldsmith, also offer training classes for coaches.

Do you need a coaching certification? For most internal positions, a coaching certification is not required, but it might be helpful in allowing you to better compete for open positions. Certification is more likely to make a difference in large companies or for external coaching practices. It is important to continually build your skills as a coach, and employers will want to see that you have taken the initiative to become exposed to a variety of resources and coaching models. As you build your coaching practice and create your personal development plan, consider a variety of training options.

Executive Coaching

Executive coaching refers to coaching provided to senior leaders, and it differs from other types of coaching in many ways. First, when coaching an executive, you will more likely need to identify and work on changing behavioral patterns. Although this may also be a component of other coaching assignments, the need for behavioral transformation for improved success will be more significant and important when coaching executives. Another difference is that executive coaches need to have an understanding of the requirements and opportunities that executives face. These can be very different and include strategy, business growth opportunities, leadership team building, influencing shareholders and boards of directors, and making complex and difficult decisions. Coaching executives is more difficult and requires you to have the strength and courage to offer direct feedback to senior leaders. Issues of confidentiality and professionalism are more important when dealing with executives because you will be exposed to proprietary and sensitive information.

Once you have fully developed your coaching practice, you may be asked to provide executive coaching. You should not attempt to do executive coaching until you have coached several dozen clients, learned how to help transform behaviors, and regularly interacted with executives. Executive coaching usually occurs over a long period of time (six months to one year), and key deliverables are agreed to in advance. According to expert executive coach Marshall Goldsmith (Morgan, Harkins, and Goldsmith, 2005), the steps for executive coaching are

- Involve the leaders being coached in determining the desired behaviors in their leadership roles.
- Involve the leaders being coached in determining key stakeholders.
- Collect feedback.
- Determine key behaviors for change.
- Have the coaching clients respond to key stakeholders.
- Review what has been learned with clients, and help them develop action plans.

Noted

"All of the behavioral coaches that I work with use the same general approach. We first get an agreement with our coaching clients and their managers on two key variables: (1) what are the key behaviors that will make the biggest positive change in increased leadership effectiveness and (2) who are the key stakeholders that should determine (one year later) if this change has occurred. We then get paid only after our coaching clients have achieved a positive change in key leadership behaviors as determined by key stakeholders." (Morgan, Harkins, and Goldsmith, 2005, p. 56).

▷ Develop ongoing follow-up processes.

▷ Review results, and start again.

Executive coaching is often outsourced. Hiring an external coach offers a level of objectivity and privacy that is highly desired. In addition, most well-regarded executive coaches have many years of experience and advanced coaching skills. Some executive coaches specialize in particular coaching issues or industries.

Getting It Done

Give small-team coaching a try. Use exercise 9-1 to select a team to approach.

Exercise 9-1. Team coaching selection worksheet.

Question	Answer
What are several teams or sub-teams with which you regularly work?	
Of these teams, which have the best relationships and mutual respect for one another?	
Do any of these teams have any major projects or initiatives on the horizon?	
Which team leaders seem most interested in developing the team's skills?	
With which team could you have the biggest effect?	
With which team do you have the best rapport and reputation?	

In the next chapter, you will learn ways to build on the information and ideas presented in this book.

10

Conclusion

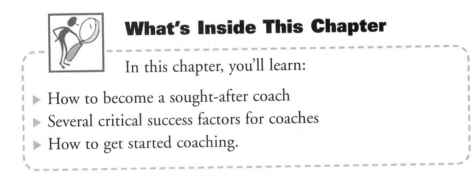

What's Inside This Chapter

In this chapter, you'll learn:

▶ How to become a sought-after coach
▶ Several critical success factors for coaches
▶ How to get started coaching.

How to Become a Sought-After Coach

Do you want your clients to seek out your coaching? Most coaches endeavor to create the reputation for being great. The ideal situation occurs when clients pull or ask for coaching (versus being pushed by managers or coaches). Think about the coaches you have sought throughout your career. What made you want to talk to and spend time with these individuals? Did they know just what to say to help you get unstuck? Could they see through your excuses and help you get back in action? Were they fun to be with? Could they whip out resources on any topic? Your clients will seek your coaching because it is a great use of their time and the experiences are positive.

Coaches offer their time to help the progress of other people. This is the essence of coaching. Coaches never try to replace their clients' goals with their own (this would become advice or counseling). Intrinsic motivation drives the best coaches to help others learn, grow, and perform. They get a charge out of helping people consider different viewpoints and enjoy seeing the proverbial lightbulb turn on for people. By helping clients move their work forward, coaches broaden their reach within and effect on the organization.

Being a coach is rewarding, but not always easy. Sometimes you will need to be willing to discuss "undiscussables" or help uncover unspoken beliefs getting in the way of your clients' goals. Your clients' beliefs or assumptions may be getting in the way of their successes. As a coach, you will help them clarify what's real and what's not (and often what's real does not matter as much as what's helpful to believe). A coach needs to be tough to hold clients accountable for realizing their goals. Doing this in a way that does not come across as bossy or directive can be tricky. The secret lies in the clarity of your intent and the strength of your relationships with your clients.

Critical Success Factors for Coaches

What separates great coaches from the rest? The answer is more basic than you might think. Here are several critical success factors for coaches:

- ▶ Great coaches are trustworthy.
- ▶ Great coaches act with integrity and follow through on agreements.
- ▶ Great coaches build positive, collaborative relationships with their clients.
- ▶ Great coaches are accessible and available.
- ▶ Great coaches know their stuff. They offer ideas that make a difference.
- ▶ Great coaches know when to be tough. Sometimes clients need a stronger nudge.
- ▶ Great coaches listen well and seek to understand and employ the assistance that their clients need most.
- ▶ Great coaches know that coaching is not about them.
- ▶ Great coaches are catalysts. They are courageous and know that it is important to say what others cannot.
- ▶ Great coaches are successful in helping clients become more coachable. This opens up many new opportunities.

- Great coaches know how to be candid in a manner that will be well received by the client.
- Great coaches love facilitating other people's successes and get a charge out of seeing the aha reaction.

These traits of great coaches develop over years of experiences. Take solace in knowing that the more you coach, the better you will likely become. Where do you get started developing your coaching practice? The short answer is that you start by coaching yourself and by coaching others. Learn by doing and ask for mentoring from experienced coaches along the way. Expert coaches who participated in a survey about coaching were asked, "What advice would you give someone who wants to learn to be a great coach?" Here are some of the responses:

- "Hire a great coach, and love people." Stewart Berman
- "Understand the sciences of human and organization development. Have years of experience doing real work so that you are able to relate more powerfully to the world of your coachee. Constantly seek ways to absorb new knowledge, enhance your skills, and acquire new ones." Mark Sobol
- "Learn from others." Bonnie S. Turner
- "The desire to be a great coach must be subjugated by the desire to serve others. A dose of humility doesn't hurt, either." Brendon Connelly
- "Get lots of feedback on your abilities as a coach, and work hard on continuous improvement." Laurence Haughton
- "Do your own work first." Vikki G. Brock
- "I work primarily in the area of leadership, which means that clients and I spend little time with tactics. Leadership requires facility in not only mental domains, but also emotional, physical, and even spiritual domains. Authentic leadership cannot be done solely through the intellect. And a coach who has little facility in domains other than mental will be of little value in that journey. The first requirement of quality coaching is the willingness and experience with their own growths." Barry Goldberg
- "Experience different coaches yourself. Read about coaching." Michael Angelo Caruso

▶ "Practice the skills, especially listening, at multiple levels. Learn all you can about the human psyche and soul. Learn all you can about your own hot buttons and projections and how you work your own agenda. Keep your ego in check." Dick Richards

▶ "Coaching is not consulting. If you want to help people with your ideas, become a consultant. If you want to lead others to discover what they can do to realize their goals, consider being a coach." Stan Herman

▶ "First, hire a coach, and learn from the person. Second, read everything you can. Third, practice a lot. Fourth, take some courses online or live. Fifth, really reflect deep inside on the true desire of being a coach. Understand the drivers and the expectations of coaching as a profession. Sixth, talk to several that specialize in different areas and different customer markets, and ask a lot of questions about their journeys." Kathy Bass

▶ "Meet other experienced coaches who have a practice that you would like to emulate. Learn from them." Marshall Goldsmith

▶ "Coaching is more about asking questions than it is about giving answers. In fact, the best thing you can do is gently lead/light the way for your clients' thinking processes to evolve, such that they come up with their own best answers and this new habit of better thinking begins to stick for them." Rosa Say

▶ "You don't know it all. You will never know it all. Make learning a corner-stone of your approach. Hire a coach. Hire a therapist. Go to workshops and seminars. Read books. Learn new approaches—new techniques. Be ever vigilant of becoming too comfortable with what you do and how you do it—that might be a sign that you're in danger of stagnation. Keep challenging yourself to expand your understanding, your awareness, and your approach." Curt Rosengren

As these experts emphasize, it is important that you seek coaching for yourself. Why? First, if you believe that coaching can make a big difference, you will want to receive that benefit yourself. Second, as you receive coaching, you will learn from your coach and better understand what your future clients will experience.

Throughout this book, you have explored many facets of coaching basics. Coaching is a service-oriented discipline focused on helping clients make their goals and dreams come true. Building strong, trusting relationships with your clients is critical and can pave the way for open and fruitful dialogue. Effective coaches help their clients get unstuck and move forward with greater velocity and influence. Enjoy coaching, and take pride in the work you do helping others do their best work!

 Getting It Done

Scan the critical success factors for coaches, and select two that you want to work on during the next month. Create two actions that you can take to develop each critical success factor.

Critical Success Factor 1:

_____

Critical Success Factor 2:

_____

References

Books

Bridges, W. (1991) *Managing Transitions.* Reading, MA: Addison-Wesley.

———. (2003). *Managing Transitions*, 2d edition. Cambridge, MA: Da Capo Press.

Burr, V. (1995). *An Introduction to Social Construction*. London: Routledge.

Caproni, P. (2001). *The Practical Coach: Management Skills for Everyday Life*. Upper Saddle River, NJ: Prentice Hall.

Carnegie, D. (1936). *How to Win Friends and Influence People*. New York: Simon and Schuster.

Coach U, Inc. (2005). *Coach U's Essential Coaching Tools: Your Complete Practice Resource*. Hoboken, NJ: John Wiley & Sons.

Ferrazzi, K. (2005). *Never Eat Alone: And Other Secrets to Success One Relationship at a Time*. With T. Raz. New York: Currency Doubleday.

Flaherty, J. (1999). *Coaching: Evoking Excellence in Others*. Burlington, MA: Butterworth-Heinemann.

Gladwell, M. (2002). *The Tipping Point: How Little Things Can Make a Big Difference*. New York: Back Bay Books/Little Brown & Company.

Morgan, H., P. Harkins, and M. Goldsmith. (2005). *The Art and Practice of Leadership Coaching: 50 Top Executive Coaches Reveal Their Secrets*. Hoboken, NJ: John Wiley & Sons.

Whitworth, L., H. Kimsey-House, and P. Sandahl. (1998). *Co-Active Coaching: New Skills for Coaching People Toward Success in Work and Life*. Mountain View, CA: Davies-Black Publishing.

Survey participants who were quoted in this book

Lora Adrianse, coach, consultant, facilitator, Essential Connections, www.connectionscoach.com.

Chris Bailey, coach, ImaginActive Coaching Resources,
    http://imaginactive.typepad.com/alchemyofsoulfulwork.
Kathy Bass, executive coach, The Executive's Edge, www.theexecutivesedge.com.
Stewart Berman, life coach, www.stewartberman.com.
Vikki G. Brock, MBA, master certified coach and certified executive coach,
    www.vikkigbrock.com.
Michael Angelo Caruso, founder and president, The Edison House,
    www.edisonhouse.com.
Brendon Connelly, director, Graduate and Professional Studies Admissions,
    www.slackermanager.com.
Barry Goldberg, Entelechy Partners, www.entelechypartners.com.
Marshall Goldsmith, founding partner, Marshall Goldsmith Partners,
    www.marshallgoldsmith.com.
Laurence Haughton, author, www.laurencehaughton.com.
Stan Herman, CEC, MBA, president, Stan Herman Inc.
Paul Lemberg, president, Quantum Growth Coaching,
    www.quantumgrowthcoaching.com.
Christina Madrid, RCC, SPHR, executive and career design coach,
    www.next-levelcoaching.com.
Carlos Marin, leadership development executive coach, www.carlosemarin.com.
John McCabe, principal, JJM Enterprises, www.jjmcoach.com.
Dave Pughe-Parry, founder of Living ADDventure, www.ladd.co.za.
Kathleen Ream, consultant.
Dick Richards, coach, consultant, author, http://ongenius.com.
Curt Rosengren, passion catalyst, http://curtrosengren.typepad.com.
Adrian Savage, coach, www.adriansavage.com.
Rosa Say, founder and head coach, Say Leadership Coaching,
    www.sayleadershipcoaching.com.
Mark Sobol, president, Leadership Strategies International, www.marksobol.com.
Bonnie S. Turner, PhD.
Tim Ursiny, PhD, CBC, RCC, founder, Advantage Coaching and Training,
    www.advantagecoaching.com.
Barry Zweibel, PCC, GottaGettaCoach! Inc., www.ggci.com.

Additional Resources

Books

Here is a list of books that will help you build your coaching library and help you learn the various practices and methods used by coaches today.

Berger, P., and T. Luckman. (1966). *The Social Construction of Reality*. New York: Anchor Books.

Blanchard, K., and D. Shula. (2001). *The Little Book of Coaching*. New York: HarperCollins.

Carson, R. (2003). *Taming Your Gremlin: A Surprisingly Simple Method for Getting Out of Your Own Way*. New York: Quill/HarperCollins.

Gergen, K. (1999). *An Invitation to Social Construction*. London: Sage Publications.

Goldsmith, M., L. Lyons, and A. Freas. (2000). *Coaching for Leadership: How the World's Greatest Coaches Help Leaders Learn*. San Francisco: Pfeiffer.

Hargrove, R. (1995). *Masterful Coaching*. San Francisco: Pfeiffer.

———. (2000). *Masterful Coaching Fieldbook*. San Francisco: Pfeiffer/Jossey Bass.

———. (1998). *Mastering the Art of Creative Collaboration*. New York: McGraw Hill.

Hargrove, R., and M. Renaud. (2004). *Your Coach in a Book*. San Francisco: Jossey Bass.

Leonard, T. (1998). *The Portable Coach*. New York: Scribner.

O'Neill, M. (2000). *Executive Coaching with Backbone and Heart: A Systems Approach to Engaging Leaders with Their Challenges*. San Francisco: Jossey Bass.

Rogers, C. (1995). *On Becoming a Person: A Therapist's View of Psychotherapy*. New York: Mariner Books.

Rothwell, W. (2000). *Effective Succession Planning: Ensuring Leadership Continuity and Building Talent From Within*. New York: American Management Association.

Stone, D., B. Patton, and S. Heen. (2000). *Difficult Conversations: How to Discuss What Matters Most.* New York: Penguin Putnam.

Winer, M., and K. Ray. (1994). *Collaboration Handbook.* St. Paul, MN: Amherst H. Wilder Foundation.

Yamashita, K., and S. Spataro. (2004). *Unstuck.* New York: Penguin Group.

Organizations and Websites

Here is a list of organizations and websites of interest to coaches.

1 to 1 Coach Training, www.1to1coachingschool.com.

Ace Project, www.aceproject.com.

American Management Association, www.amanet.org.

American Society for Training and Development, www.astd.org.

Career Coach Institute, www.careercoachinstitute.com.

Coach Training University, www.coachtraininguniversity.com.

Coach U, www.coachinc.com/coachu.

FranklinCovey, www.franklincovey.com.

Goal Maker Software, www.goalmaker.com.

GoalPro, www.goalpro.com.

International Coach Federation, www.coachfederation.org.

Life Plan Writer, www.lifeplanwriter.com.

ManagePro, www.managepro.com.

Single-step, www.single-step.com.

About the Author

Lisa Haneberg has been a coach for 22 years. Her experience includes work for and with companies like Intel Corporation, Black & Decker, Mead Paper, Amazon.com, Beacon Hotel Corporation, Cruise West, and Travcoa. She is the author of *H.I.M.M. (High Impact Middle Management): Solutions for Today's Busy Managers, Organization Development Basics*, and numerous articles and e-books. Haneberg writes a management blog called Management Craft and regularly writes about coaching. She has a bachelor's degree in behavioral sciences; completed graduate work in organization development and human resources; attended many professional training courses; and received certifications in the areas of coaching, facilitation, training, and behavioral tendencies assessment tools. Haneberg lives in Seattle, Washington, and has a consulting firm called Haneberg Management. For more information or to contact Lisa Haneberg, go to www.haneberg-management.com or email lhaneberg@gmail.com.